YOUR RELATIONSHIP RESCUE HANDBOOK

11 "F" Words to Increase the Love

Jim Hetherington

10-10-10
Publishing

Your Relationship Rescue Handbook:
11 "F" Words to Increase the Love
Hetherington, Jim

ISBN-13: 978-1725626263
ISBN-10: 1725626268

Published by: 10-10-10 Publishing
Markham, Ontario

First 10-10-10 Publishing paperback edition

Contents

I dedicate this book to every person, and couple,
that longs for a deep and intimate relationship,
with a loving and compassionate partner.

And to my wonderful wife, Mary,
with whom I've grown and shared life's journey,
for over 36 years. Your commitment and belief in me,
even when I struggled to see it, is a true inspiration.
Thank you for loving me and making it
so easy to love you back.

Foreword

If you want to be in a long-term relationship, you need all the help you can get. Getting started and being prepared are vital elements to your success.

Jim's approach in *Your Relationship Rescue Handbook* is practical, informative and encouraging. This book will help you see your life in a whole new way.

I believe the 11 "F" words he uses in this book are vital to you. They touch on the key areas that you may fail to talk about or even consider when you are entering into a relationship. Most of these areas are in your life but you may give little thought to what you truly believe about each of them. Until now, that is. This book will bring new awareness and language to key topics that you may not have thought were that important.

Your Relationship Rescue Handbook is a great resource for you, as you start to think about these things and form your own sense of value; what you believe and stand for. This book is also a great tool for you, if you are part of a couple who is just starting out. You can use this book as a guide to form your own plan of action and become united in your approach together. It is also helpful, even if you have been married for a long time, to take these principles and have the discussions all over again (or perhaps for the first time), and stay on track to a long, healthy marriage.

Jim's experience as a coach, mentor, teacher, trainer and author are evident throughout the pages of this book. He shares some of his and others' stories, and gives sound ideas that will make you rethink your approach to marriage and relationships.

You need to work hard to have a "Happy Ever After" and I'm confident you will find the "F" words in this book great tools to move you forward to that end.

To your healthy and happy relationship,

Raymond Aaron
New York Times Bestselling Author

Testimonial

My friendship with Jim Hetherington goes back almost 30 years, from the time that he and his family first joined the church I was pastoring in Canada. Jim and his wife, Mary, led our youth ministry for a number of years. They were outstanding leaders. I was able to assess Jim's ministry both as a parent and as the senior pastor. He and Mary were confident, affirming and compassionate, able to set clear boundaries and create a remarkably positive atmosphere for the youth.

Years later, Jim took me to Nicaragua where he connected me with a major church leader. Jim's initiative has led to multiple mission trips and many humanitarian projects, impacting thousands of lives. He co-led a large team where, once again, he demonstrated excellent leadership.

Jim is a clear communicator, an excellent listener, and an effective and creative processor. Most of all, he is a man of great integrity. It is a privilege to recommend this book to everyone.

Steve Stewart
CEO, Impact Nations

Acknowledgements

The writing of this book has been a lengthy process. It started a few decades ago as I spent countless hours mentoring and teaching youth and young adults. The years of teaching them has taught me valuable lessons as well. Over the years, I have seen the importance of knowing who we are and what we believe in. The principles in this book, in part, have been developed through the investment in their lives.

I want to acknowledge my wife, Mary, my son, Aaron, and daughter, Sarah: you were with me on this journey as I discovered who I really am; and even when I didn't always show my best, you still loved me. You are such a blessing to me, and I am truly thankful for you. A husband and father couldn't ask for a better family than you were, and continue to be today.

To my Dad and Mom, Victor and Joanne, you never gave up on me, even when I quit high school before I completed it. I know you were disappointed, but you stuck with me and encouraged me. You gave me freedom, more than I deserved, to find myself and grow towards being the man I am today. Who would have thought that the teenager that quit high school, because he hated to read, would now be writing books? Thanks for always loving and supporting me.

Even though I left school early, there were countless mentors in my life who have encouraged me along the way. Robert Duthie, you helped me, as a young, uneducated husband and father, make sense of things and find direction. Derek Perry, who sat with me one Saturday afternoon and taught me how to truly read, and to retain knowledge as I started on a new journey to learn and better myself.

Steve Stewart, you were an example of leadership to me like no other. You showed me by example what it was to be a leader and help people grow to be their best. You created a vacuum that drew me in to be a better person, just from your influence. And you invested a quarter and made a telephone call to invite me on a journey of compassion with you, which brought me up out of a time of great despair in my life. I haven't forgotten that, and I haven't stopped learning and growing to be a better man since you made that call. Thank you.

There are countless friends and family members who have encouraged me along the way; and, of course, it has helped me to be where I am today. If I tried to make a list of everyone, I know I would miss someone, and I don't want to do that. So, thank you, friends and family.

I have had the privilege of leading many short-term mission trips to Central America. Dave and Liz Cabot, Pastor Osvaldo and Rosy Bonilla, and my many friends and family in Nicaragua, thank you for allowing me to serve, teach, and share with you over all these years. And thank you for showing me the true meaning of friendship and sacrificial giving. You are all amazing!

I'm especially thankful for the wisdom I receive. I recognize that it comes from God, and only by grace do I have it. My desire is to be a vessel to share with many.

1

Starting Your Journey

Is it even possible to have a *Happy Ever After* anymore? Many people ask themselves this more and more. After all, it happens in the movies; it's in the lyrics of love songs; and it can be read about in books—it must be possible. However, with the demands placed on us from running our businesses, building careers, working, and life, it's getting harder and harder with each passing year to maintain balance in every area of life, and to work on our *happily ever after.* What about young couples just starting out? What chance do they have in building long-term, lasting relationships? With divorce rates skyrocketing, domestic disputes a common occurrence, and the fact that everyone seems to have an "I want it all and I want it now" attitude, it's becoming more challenging to keep a healthy marriage and long-term relationships.

One of the top 10 reasons for divorce is because of not being prepared. Many of us are encouraged to follow our hearts when it comes to love. Friends and family counsel us with the "Do they make you happy?" script. Of course, they make you happy. Everyone is happy at first. But what preparation is made to have lasting, outstanding relationships? And what do we do once we are in a long-term relationship, to keep it current and real?

For almost three decades, I have counselled and mentored youth and young adults in life and relationships. Often, when a young couple had found each other, out of the billions of people on the planet, they would come to me to share the new found love they had discovered. They would tell me that they're in love and are convinced that this is "the one," and want to make it the best thing ever. I usually start the conversation with the same questions: Is this person taking you toward the goals and the plan you have for your life, or are they taking you from it?

If you have a vision for your life and know where you want to go, the last thing you need is to get into a relationship with someone who will slow you down or keep you from achieving those goals—or worse, take you off track all together.

The next thing I ask is, what do your friends and family think? Often times, people get into relationships where everyone else can tell, straight away, that it's not right. But we've got blinders on; it's called love (Or maybe it's really infatuation?), and we don't see clearly. But the people around us, who know us, can see it clearly. Our ability to discern is clouded when we're in love, and we need to rely on those close friends and family members to help us see. We need to be surrounded with people who will speak the truth into our lives, and we need to be willing to receive it from them. We can't go with our feelings and our gut all the time. We need to have trusted people in our lives, who will give it to us straight and honest. However, we need to make sure that they aren't people who are going to tell us what we want to hear just to make us happy. We all know and have people around us that are like this, and we need to be sure that we are selecting people who are going to be honest and straight forward with us.

If God is important to our lives, then we need to be open to spiritual direction. If we really want to honour God, friends, and family, and ultimately ourselves, it's important to look at all these things. If all these things check out, then I would encourage them to take things slow, and to grow a healthy trust and relationship together.

I think it wise to start the dating, or courting, with trusted people around us, so that they can see how you interact with your new partner. This will serve a couple in two ways: First, it will give you a safe place, a guarded place, where you can get to know each other and see the real character of each other as it comes out. Your date will realize that it's not only you that they need to impress, but your *tribe* also. It will keep a man or woman on their best behaviour as they are getting to know you and getting to know those you trust and respect at the same time. As you get to know this person, you then begin to spend time alone and see if the way they treat you with your friends is the same when they are alone with you. You want to be treated the same in private as you are in public. A lot can be determined about a person by how they act or treat you in private, when they don't have to pretend, and nobody is watching. This is extremely helpful when starting a new relationship, and even as it develops. It's a good idea to keep your self surrounded with people you know and trust.

So often, a person will begin to treat us differently as they get to know us. We don't always treat the ones closest to us with the highest respect all the time. We'll talk more about this in later chapters.

We all know that many of our so called *love of my life* relationships don't last long, and we go on to the next. As years have gone by, I have put together a list of areas that I feel are important in order to develop a healthy relationship. These principles can also be useful in putting together a check list that can help identify a person who would be more suitable for us long term. I've taught this over the years to people, but it has sometimes been met with resistance and blocked ears.

The problem I see is that many are interested in solutions to problems, and not solutions to prevent problems down the road. When we're in love, the quirky little things that the other may do don't bother us. However, soon into the relationship, or perhaps years into it, those same things drive us crazy. We begin to see red when they do those cute little things: things like smacking their lips when they eat, picking their teeth at the table after a meal, making insensitive comments, or…. There are countless things that can set us over the edge.

Now, I'm not suggesting that the areas we are going to discuss in the book will solve all the problems and prevent bad things from happening; sometimes the quirky things are going to get us. Squeezing the toothpaste in the middle of the tube, or leaving the toilet seat up all the time, may bother us whether we take the time to discover Mr. or Mrs. Right, or not. What I am suggesting is, if we take the time to discuss the areas we will look at in this book, before we get married, and use this to continue the dialogue after, then these areas don't need to be points of friction in our marriage and relationships.

The process to build a long-term relationship starts long before we get into one, and it doesn't stop even after we are in a relationship. The structure of this book can help in three ways:

Young adults and youth can begin to apply these principles and build a list of the kind of person that they want in their life. Growing up is a perfect time to compare different personalities, traits, and general appearances that they find attractive or repelling. It's a great time to observe how people get along and what kind of person is most appealing. As they mature, they will have a good idea of the person that they are interested in, and they will have a better sense of who they are, what they want, and where they are going. As they form a clearer sense of who they are, using these principles, they can begin to project that confidence and attract the person they want in their life.

Couples that are considering marriage can take these principles and begin to have conversations; they can discuss them and come to consensus with their significant other. Not only that, but they can use them to clearly define who they are and what they believe. Moving forward, couples can use these items to build their own purpose statement, and build a long-term relationship with these principles, as well as having a reference to come back to when there is a dispute. Clearly defined purposes and values are a great place to come back to as a tool to keep a marriage or relationship on track.

Married couples, or those in a long-term relationship, can use these as a starting point to decide on next steps. It can be challenging to maintain a relationship today and to balance business and home life. These areas are great tools to use to discuss the things that are important and the things that aren't. If you have never written a purpose statement, it's not too late. And if you haven't discussed the areas in this book, it's not too late for that either; use these areas, and start now. Add the values and principles that are important to you both and build one. You'll begin to share a common vision that will only help, moving forward.

Over the years, I've sat across the table from many couples discussing their upcoming marriage and their wedding plans. The conversation always starts with, "Congratulations," and then is followed with, "How did you meet?" I love hearing the stories of how people have met, the way love has developed, and how and when it became real to them as a couple. I'll then give some words of advice and encourage them through our dialogue. Quite often, the topic will inevitably turn to the topics in this book. I'm convinced that the more we know what our personal convictions are with these "F" words, and the more that the person we are in relationship with knows their convictions—if they match—our compatibility will be greater.

I'm passionate about sharing and teaching these principles, and helping couples discuss these topics to build a stronger foundation in the relationship. As I mentioned earlier, when I share these ideas, they usually respond with the response, "Oh, we're good." I'll ask about plans of having a family, and sometimes I get a clear idea of what they're thinking; but it's often, "We're going to wait and see what happens," or, "We're not sure yet." It's these kinds of answers that concern me, because the couple hasn't discussed a very important topic. One or the other could be in for a surprise, especially if one wants children and the other doesn't.

What really drove this home for me, and solidified the importance of discussing these principles, was one couple I sat with. We met and were talking about their upcoming wedding ceremony and the details of the service. While talking, they asked a question or two about my marriage, and we started a very lengthy, heart-to-heart conversation. There was discussion of finances and friendships. We talked about preferring one another and encouraging each other to be the very best person that they both know they are called to be. Also, about how it is each other's responsibility to grow as a person and to help the other grow as well. While we were talking, I noticed tears rolling down the cheek of the bride-to-be. I stopped and asked if everything was okay. She looked at me, wiped her face, and said, "No one has ever talked to me like this. No one has ever shared these ideas with me before. I'm twenty-four years old, and I've never heard this before."

It was then that I realized it was necessary to write this book, with the ideas and thoughts to help individuals discover what they believe, and to help couples build a strong foundation.

At the time of writing this book, I have been married to my best friend, Mary, for 36 years. I've raised two wonderful children: Aaron, my oldest, and Sarah. I wish I had more of these principles refined when I was a younger husband and father. My wife and children have grown through a lot of the testing and developing ground of these principles, but they will tell you we did well together as a family. Mary, my wife, will agree with me when I say that for the first twelve years of our relationship, we were still trying to mesh and find common ground on a lot of things. The key, however, was that we decided right from the beginning of our marriage that we would not entertain the "D" word: Divorce. We were in it for the long run and were determined to work and struggle through our differences. Often times, struggles are just that—differences or communication issues—all which can be worked on. We set ourselves up for a win-win situation. We both wanted to succeed in life and marriage.

When two people come together in marriage, both sides have baggage. By that, I mean that each of us brings things into the relationship: the way we were raised, with the unique set of values that we had growing up. Our life experiences, our hurts, failures, and disappointments contribute to how we enter into relationships and marriage. All that is in us. And when we unite in marriage, we are both coming from the set of values that we developed growing up. Good or bad, these values and mindsets are there, and we approach our relationship from those perspectives.

Think of it like two baseball teams. We have some idea of how the game is played, but because we had different coaches and trainers, our approach to the game may be slightly different.

You may not like the way I hold my bat. I may not like the way you crowd the plate when you're up to bat. Subtle differences to the same game can cause irritation or aggravation. Don't believe me? Just watch a championship game and see how aggravated the players get with each other, because they are playing for a bigger prize. They want the calls to go their way. They will argue and dispute every little thing because they don't want to lose. It's the same in marriage. Now that you're married and in a long-term relationship, the stakes are higher. You're playing for a different goal. You both want to win, but with your set of ideals and values. If they differ slightly, and they will, you'll get at each other's throat because you think your values are right and the other is wrong. Sometimes you just want to win—win every argument, every dispute, or fight—you don't want to lose, and the tension can build as you discuss things.

There is a different way. You can both work on the rule book, and together, write a script that will work for you both. You can share values and common goals and objectives. You can create a plan and refer back to it often, and even adjust and modify as you go along. The important thing is this: Be on the same page. That is the page you write for your long-term relationship. Create your own values statement. Your own goals statement. Your own purpose statement.

Another tool I suggest to my coach clients and couples I meet with, is the Kolbe test. When you take the Kolbe test you go through a series of multiple choice questions. You are instructed to answer them as if you had perfect freedom to do things the way you want and how you want. The results are amazing. It divides the results into four areas; fact finder, follow through, quick start and implementer. From this test you will see why and how you do things and your partner as well. If you're single, take it so you better understand yourself and you will see the type of person you should pursue. As a couple it will be so helpful in your overall relationship. I can't say enough about it. If you want to find out more go to my website www.YourRelationship RescueCoach.com and you'll find the link there. If we apply some tools and principles that we both agree on, then we can get to a healthier relationship faster and have a more enjoyable ride along the way. It doesn't make sense to just set things up with our principles and values. You will need to visit them yearly, or maybe more often, to be sure they are still current, and that you both agree where things are going. So, let's dive in and begin to look at the "F" words in your relationship, and see how they can shape things up.

What word will we talk about first?

Jim Hetherington

Thoughts

2

Faith

Today, in many parts of the world, people are living in multicultural societies. And there is a greater sense of acceptance today in many countries toward religion, culture, and ethnic background. There is a real desire by many to experience other cultures and to embrace diversity today; and young people are growing up together and sharing their different cultural and religious ideas and beliefs. For many, the conversation of religious or spiritual beliefs doesn't come up. They just accept everyone for who they are and don't give the topic much consideration.

Growing up, all of us are shaped by the beliefs, or lack of beliefs, in our immediate family circle. Our mom and dad, or guardian, may have had certain traditions and beliefs, and as young children, we were required to follow their beliefs and standards. For some of us, we may have enjoyed it and gave ourselves 100% to the beliefs that our parents introduced us to. Or, it may have been our grandparents who had a sense of direction and introduced it to us; and we loved the times we spent with them and the investment they made in us, and we still follow those traditions and teachings today.

On the flip side, we may have had parents, guardians, or grandparents that forced their traditions and beliefs on us, and we may resent it and have nothing to do with those traditions today. It may have been torture for us to follow them when deep inside we could easily think of a thousand other things we would rather be doing. Then the day came for us to make up our own mind and decide which way we were going. We chose whether to stay and follow the traditions we grew up with or to stay away from traditions and do our own thing.

When I was a young boy, my parents took me and my three siblings to church every Sunday. I remember going to a restaurant after, for Sunday lunch, and it almost always included my favourite drink, a Coke float. Holidays were marked with special memories and fondness, and I can still picture many of those events and the people I knew from those days.

As I grew, the services became boring and unimportant to me, and I slowly began to fight my parents most Sundays as they requested my attendance. Eventually, I remember having the conversation with them that as long as I went on the special holidays, like Christmas, Easter, Mother's and Father's Day, the other Sundays were up to me whether I went or not. So, of course, I started to go less and less, until I stopped all together.

I experienced some troubling times in my late teens, and after fighting with my parents, and experiencing many of life's tempting adventures, I did return to the belief structure that my parents introduced me to as a young boy. Around the same time, I met a young lady; and after a short time, we recognized that we shared the same beliefs. Within a year of meeting, we got married, and shortly after that, we had two children. Now, as parents, we introduced them to the same things, and they eventually chose the path they wanted to follow.

Even though I didn't always want to follow my parents and

do the things they were doing, or believe the things that they believed, something was shaping me, although I didn't see it. People all around us are being shaped by the things learned as children and throughout adulthood. These beliefs go with us in all of our relationships. You may have been raised with no real spiritual guidance, but inside, you do have a belief system. There are things that you feel strongly about, and there are things that you like or dislike. There might be things that you would follow or believe that someone else wouldn't.

The point here is that all people, regardless of how we are raised, develop a belief system. It doesn't matter how we got it. We may receive it from formal training at a church or synagogue, or from the streets, or from TV. Regardless of where, we are all shaped, and we form our own faith. A structure develops in us, and it becomes what we stand for. This can be particularly dangerous if we were hurt or wounded in our upbringing, because we may blame that structure for what happened to us, and vow to never have anything to do with it again.

People get wounded by leadership all the time. It can be in a church, at a kid's club, school club, or anywhere. People can also disagree with leadership at any time. One of the hazards of being a leader is that they have to make decisions, and people aren't going to like some of those decisions. Some people will walk away from an institution and never return because of the decisions leaders make.

It can even be political. We may disagree with a certain member of parliament, or we may not like a particular leader in our country. And we may carry that prejudice toward that person or a political party, and it may carry over to our children or those we have influence over. Having a political view is fine. Having a view about a religion or another organization is fine. The difficulty is, when we have children, they can begin to pick up on our views, right or wrong. Many people, today, make their decision of religion or politics based on what they pick up from parents rather than from facts and truth; that's both sad and scary. We make too many choices on others' opinions, and not on truth.

Then there are people who don't talk about these things at all—like the old expression: "Never talk religion or politics with anybody." And that's what happens; we don't talk about these things. We think that our faith is private and that it doesn't need to be shared.

However, what if the person we grow in love with has completely opposite views on things than we do? What if you never cross the line and discuss the area of faith? Then you get married, only to discover that their belief system is completely different than yours. Beliefs and cultural standards may dictate that men and women act a certain way or do certain things. What if you discovered, after you were married, that your partner had a deal-breaker, based on their beliefs?

It's important to talk about this area, to know where each other is coming from, for several reasons.

First, it makes for a more harmonious relationship. If both sides are on the same side of the fence, it makes communication easier. It makes holiday and family times a whole bunch smoother when you share the same views. You have peace of mind and unity. You will have less resentful gatherings. If one person believes in a holiday tradition, and the other doesn't, there is a lot of tension and displeasure around the table.

Secondly, if you plan on having children after you get married, how important is it to you that both of you share the same values and beliefs when it comes to raising children? Having children brings with it a whole set of responsibilities. You are now in a position where you will shape and influence that young life. The things you believe and value are going to be instilled into your children. If you and your partner have different views or beliefs, how will that affect your child? How will that affect discipline, education, and the values you teach in the home. If parents are divided on issues, then the child has no clear direction or vision; and it's important that now, more than ever, the home be a united and safe place.

Children will notice if respect is reciprocated between parents. They are very sensitive and aware of what's going on in their environment. Having Mom and Dad respect and love each other is vital to a successful home. Parents can't sit back and do nothing, and just say, "Well, we are going to let them decide what they believe when they grow up." Children need a system, now. They need to understand right and wrong while growing up. They need structure, order, and values as they grow up, not just when they are older.

By then, their ideals will be so wildly shaped that they may never really make any clear educated decisions. As parents, we have an obligation to raise children in an environment free and void of as many prejudices that may have caused us to make poor choices. They need to have the freedom to make decisions, by having all the facts in front of them. Then they can make rational choices, from qualifying facts, and not the misguided ideals of parents who have been hurt and wounded.

Growing up, I never saw my parents argue in front of us kids. Never. I know that they didn't always agree on everything all the time, but I can never remember them arguing, yelling, or bad mouthing each other in front of us. They would always discuss things in private. Now, that's not to say home life was perfect; but looking back, I can see the value that Mom and Dad instilled in us by not subjecting us to their verbal lashing in public.

Looking back at it now, I see the comfort and security it

brought to me. The fact that Mom and Dad had the same values, respected each other, and shared the same beliefs when it came to instructing, disciplining, and teaching values, we knew what to expect all the time.

Can you begin to see the importance of this area and the need to discuss it? Everything that we believe, affects us and the people we are in close relationship with. Their beliefs will have some influence in our life and the life of our children as they grow, because our beliefs motivate our thinking and the way we act and respond to things.

Third, the friends and family of our partner may have more of an impact on things than we may think. We probably have a friend or a family member that we can think of that takes things to the next level when it comes to passion about something. We may believe something and be serious about it, but this friend or family member is extreme. They take things to a whole new level.

Take sports, for example. We all know a friend or family member that has to eat the same foods, wear the same clothes, and sit in the same spot when they come over for an important sports game. Or the relative that is extra passionate about politics and will argue and debate anything and everything. I mean, we've all seen or experienced situations like this. Now, if we apply this thinking to faith, you can see where I'm going with this.

In the realm of faith, there may be friends or family members that believe strongly in the values upheld in a particular faith. There may not be any grey areas in their views—only black and white. And they may live it out in an entirely passionate level. If these friends or family members are close to your partner, then they may influence their thinking. Your partner may become more extreme in their views and become as passionate as that friend or family member. So, friends and family can have a great influence in our lives. The things today that seem unimportant may well become very important and influential down the road.

It's important, therefore, that the discussion around faith is held so that both sides know where the other is coming from. If you were raised with the belief that someone's faith is private, and is their business and no one else's, I'm suggesting that that is not a good approach. The way someone believes is entirely up to the individual; however, if you're hitching yourself to them, as it were, then you need to know what you're hitching up to. In a sense, their beliefs and values will directly influence you, and you need to know what they are.

It's important that you, as an individual, know what you believe, and to make sure that you and your partner's beliefs are on point. One friend said to me once, "If you don't stand for something, you'll fall for anything." You need to know what it is you believe in so that you can stand if challenged and stand by your convictions. You need to know what they are.

You need to remember that eventually the road you travel with your faith will intersect with the person you are closest to. The topic of faith can't be avoided because at some point in you're life a crisis will come and you will want to express your faith or call on your faith. The beliefs that you and your partner share will cross at some point. It may as well be earlier than later in the relationship. When the crisis come you want them in your corner, not opposing you.

I shared, earlier, how I attended church when I was young but then got away from going to church in my teens. When I met my wife, I was still at the stage of just going for the important church events and holiday times, and that was it. She, on the other hand, was a regular attendee. She invited me to go with her to her church one morning. Wanting to know what she believed in, and to know the friends and influencers in her life, I accepted the invitation.

The first thing I learned was that her church didn't meet in a traditional church building but rather a school. *A school,* I thought, *What kind of self-respecting church meets in a school?* I was raised in a very traditional, conservative church. The kind of church that even if they were being held up and robbed on Sunday morning, they wouldn't raise their hands. But wanting to know, I went.

It was a shock at first, with all the hand raising and swinging. But we got through that, and over time, started to spend more time at a place of worship we could both appreciate. We could have locked horns and both dug in our heels, with one going one way and the other one heading off in the opposite direction, but we discussed it and adjusted, and made a plan.

Now sometimes people change throughout the relationship and pick up new ideas and things that they want to follow. That happens. The thing to do here is twofold. If your partner is the one who has changed, and you find it challenging, then speak to them and find the common ground. It's no good going around slamming cupboard doors and bad mouthing your partner to any set of ears that will listen. And if you are the one who has changed, then lighten up. You're not going to reorder the whole world over night, so just relax and enjoy each other; get used to the new thing in your life and adjust.

If either one of you has introduced a new element to the marriage or relationship, you need to respect your partner. Because you are bringing a brand-new thing in the mix, you need to be respectful and not expect them to agree with this new thing right away. It may take some time. They may need to see how this is really working for you. They may want to see some positive change in your life before they join in. There can't be an introduction of something new, especially if you have known each other for a while. Let's say you've been together for 10 years, and then, overnight, you take on a new faith view. It would be unreasonable to expect them to just agree with you and get on board.

Our faith is important to us—no matter what we believe. Our faith represents our future hope, our salvation, our values, our belief structures, our confidence, our security, our peace, and so on. No matter what we believe, we don't want our beliefs threatened or compromised.

We want to believe and have faith in what we believe, as we believe. Wouldn't it follow that we would want to surround ourselves with like-minded people? Wouldn't it follow that we have our closest friend and lover be of the same mind?

If you love the outdoors as I do, and you enjoy going for walks and exploring, you want to surround yourself with like-minded people. You're going to express your love for nature, and your life choices reflect that. Would you hang around with people that hate nature, destroy the planet, and who don't care about it at all? No! You're getting around people that share the same passion, and you're enjoying life together. It's the same with politics, world issues, family values, fair trade, and so on. There are limits to the relationship that we will have with others that don't agree with our position.

With faith, it's even more important for us to have the closest person to us share similar values and ideals.

Having faith in something or someone greater than ourselves is amazing. The sad thing would be allowing ourselves to get into a relationship with someone who believes completely opposite of what we do.

As I mentioned earlier, sometimes people change. You may start out on the same page with your partner, but one of you jumps ship and starts to believe something different. What to do? One thing that could be done is to write a mission statement, as a couple, that would include the things that are important to you: all your values and important issues that you both stand for.

Start with a blank piece of paper, and begin to ask each other what the most important things are. Start with your faith. What do you believe as a couple? What would you want to teach your children? You can create a whole sentence or paragraph that describes what you believe, and why. It would include the faith organization, if you attend one, and some of the values that they hold, which appeal to you both. If you attend a church, for example, there must be a reason you are attracted to that particular church. So, if it's important enough for you to attend and commit time and energy to, then it must be important to your overall position as a couple. Then, you may start to write down things that you value, like friendships and family. Begin to discuss the boundaries that you want to have when offering help, for example. It's great to want to help a friend or family member that needs help, but what limits will you put in place so that you don't overextend yourselves? You know the old expression, about what friends and garbage have in common: after three days, they both begin to stink. While it may be important to your faith to help out, you need to have good boundaries in place in your own mission statement that outlines what you will and won't do.

You want to include as many things in this statement as you feel is important, so that you have something to come back to for reference. The whole purpose of this exercise is to have a document that you both created. You can look at it when a situation comes up, and ask, "Is what we are doing here now, in line with our mission statement?" When either of you starts to go off track of this vision you created, you can look at it and see how things are lining up. It can be changed any time you both feel it needs to be changed. You can add or subtract, shift and delete, anything, anytime. The point of this statement is for you both to have a common vision and a place to discuss and grow from.

For more details on how to create your mission statement go to my website at www.YourRelationshipRescueCoach.com.

It's like joining a sports team. If you decide that you want to play a sport, you learn the basic rules before you start playing, so that you have an idea of what's going on. You will learn the finer points as you go, but you want to have an idea of how to engage in the sport before you get going. A long-term relationship is the same thing. Create the rules, the guide lines, and the boundaries, so that you both know how to engage.

Faith has been linked to longevity of life. Those in a faith-based community can live longer, happier, and healthier lives. There is something about being connected to a larger community. Having people around us to support us and encourage us brings a sense of calmness and peace to our lives. It's knowing that we are not alone, and it's knowing that we can have people to call on, no matter what.

And it's also having the knowledge or the awareness of something bigger than us to draw from. Knowing that there is a God, a Creator, connects us to the world and to the Universe in a powerful way. There is a peace and a calmness that comes to us as we spend time communicating with our Creator, and meditating.

Somebody that lives in despair, and walks in fear all the time, brings stress to their body; therefore, poor health can be the result. Somebody that is weighed down by the worries of life, and is fearful of the future, will find it difficult to have a healthy outlook and a healthy body. However, someone who walks with peace and confidence and assurance will certainly have a healthier body.

Now, I know genetics can play a role on both sides here, but on average, as science has looked at these people, they have found that those who have faith, often live happier, healthier, and fuller lives.

People with strong faith have strong love, and often have strong convictions. Again, there is something powerful about people who live in a faith community. They look out for each other; they care for each other, and they are there for each other.

As we talked earlier, I think it's important for people looking to get into a relationship to know what they value and believe in, and that they seek to attract a like-minded person. People who are already in a long-term relationship or marriage need to discuss faith and come to a place where both sides agree. As any relationship develops and grows, having a faith-based relationship, and one that both sides agree on, will make everybody live happier and healthier.

Are you ready to look into the next word?

Thoughts

.

3

Family

We've already discussed how family shapes us. Many of the things we believe, or don't believe, come from many of the circumstances we had growing up. Influences from what we learn growing up shape us from the inside out.

It's been said that you can't choose your family. You can choose your friends; you can choose the people you associate with, but you can't choose your family.

And it's also true that you can't choose the family that you were born into. By now, we realize that there is no such thing as the stork, and we didn't get dropped at the wrong place by accident. Each of us has been born into the family that we have, and we have to deal with the cards we've been given.

Good or bad, rich or poor, in sickness or in health—it almost sounds a bit like marriage vows—but that's what we've been given, and that's what we have to accept. We all need to put up with the crazy uncles and the chatty aunts that come along with each family. There are also the genetic issues. In each family, some are tall and some are short; some are large and some are thin. Some have good cholesterol and some have bad cholesterol; and some have hair and some don't.

There are some things in our family lines that we can change. Even though we're born into certain geographic locations and economic positions, we can change that with hard work. By applying ourselves, getting more training, and moving, we can secure better jobs and place ourselves in better environments.

We can see that certain things in a family can be changed. A lot of things cannot. Our mother will always be our mother; our father will always be our father. Our brothers and sisters— they're there as well. The one thing we do have influence over is what family we get married into.

It gives us a great advantage to be able to look at a family from the outside and decide whether we want to be a part of it. We have the opportunity to look at the mom and dad, the brothers and sisters, the aunts, and the uncles; and we could decide whether we want to be a part of that family or not. When we are dating, or getting to know someone, that's the time to really have a hard look at the family structure that we could be marrying into.

Through the process of getting to know somebody, this is the critical time to really look at what we could be getting ourselves into. Before we make any hasty decision, we really need to look at the family line that we're about to get connected to. Have a look at the parents of the person you are interested in. Your future partner is likely to be similar to the parents. They would likely be like their mother or their father, or maybe their grandparents. So, what you see in the parent is usually what the person will be like down the road.

There are a large number of influences that happened in our life growing up. From when we were young, our parents have been shaping us by everything that they say or do. The things that they have taught us have shaped us into the person that we are. We have been shaped by the way we've been disciplined and the way we've been taught all through our years of growing up at home. Everything that we were allowed to do, or were not allowed to do, has shaped us one way or the other. The things that we were exposed to growing up—for example, the books, the TV shows, the friends we were allowed to hang out with— all had an influence in the way we were raised.

If one of our parents had a phobia or a fear, it may influence the way we are today. If we had parents with strong political or religious beliefs, that would certainly influence the way we are today. And it's the same with any person that we're interested in having a relationship with. All the family members that they were around when they were raised, have influenced their thinking and the way they are. That's why I say it's important to look at the family that you want to invest in—because their past may dictate what that person is going to be like.

There is also the genetics. Family lines can carry physical illnesses: things like heart-related illnesses, and so many other things as well. Not that these are things to run away from but certainly things that we want to be aware of.

So much baggage can be brought into the relationship from both sides, and that's worth having a look at.

Can you think back and recall a traumatic event from your childhood? Or does your partner talk of events from the past? Do either of you have family members who talk of past events?

As we become aware of these, I think it's important that we have a hard look at these situations and see how they may be affecting things today, or how they could affect things moving forward. Each of us should take a good hard look at our own family. Look at the things that our grandparents did, for example, and see if there's any influence in our life from them. They may have grown up during the war and have seen some terrible things. They may have grown up during times when things were very difficult, and there may be habits or fears that have been projected onto the next generations. If they grew up in a time where there was political unrest in their country, there may be great suspicions that they passed on to us toward government and officials. Even our attitude towards policing can be influenced by those around us.

And then, look at our parents. What influence did their parents have on them that they may be passing on to us? Take time and think back on different stages in your life, and see if there are ways that your parents have influenced your thinking in a negative way. What kind of dialogue is going on in our heads automatically because of the way we've been raised? There might be suspicions that we have towards certain people or certain political parties, and we don't know where that came from. By taking time to reflect on those things, it will help us moving forward, and help identify any baggage that we may be carrying.

Sometimes we just do things because that's the way our parents did it.

For example, I heard a story of a daughter who watched her mother cooking a roast beef on Sunday morning. The mother took the roast, unwrapped it and cut the ends off of the roast. She then placed it in the roasting pan. The daughter was curious and asked her mom why she cut the ends of the roast off. She simply replied that that's how my mother did it. Now, the mother was curious, and so she asked her mother why she did that. It turned out that her mother had an extra-large roast one time, and it wouldn't fit in her roasting pan. She cut off the ends so it would fit into the only pan that she had.

That was the only reason; the roast was just simply too big for the roasting pan.

How many things could we be doing in our lives that may not be necessary?

How many habits have we formed just because it was the example that was given us?

Examining our own lives as we mature is a good habit to get into. Examine why we do the things that we do. From this examination, if we do this often, we will form good healthy habits. As we do this, we form a good sense of who we are as an individual. We develop a strong sense of good habits and strong values, and when we have this in ourselves, we project that forward into our future relationships.

As we are dating someone, and we're getting to know them, observe things that are going on in the family dynamic. Some things, like cutting off the end of a roast, are easy to deal with and can be changed. However, deeper cultural issues in family lines may not be as easy to adjust. As I mentioned earlier, in the faith chapter, there can be many different cultural and religious beliefs that may be harder to adapt to. If we have the conviction to live a free and open life, and the one that we see in a future partner's family dynamic doesn't line up with our convictions, then we may want to consider what we are doing. Certain religions or cultures have ideals that they expect family members to carry out. This could be an issue that you would want to look at before the relationship goes deeper. If it's something that goes by and isn't discussed, then it may become a deeper issue as the relationship goes on. Remember, you can't choose your family, but you can choose the one you enter into.

If you are in a family dynamic where there is tension over family structures because of religious or cultural values, sit down with your partner and go through them together. Look at the values and go through them one by one, and see if you can find common ground, from where you can agree and start fresh.

Don't take each issue personal, or go on the attack or become very defensive. Rather, sit down at a table across from one another and discuss the issues. If you find as you discuss the issues that one or both of you feel like you're being attacked you may want to place an object on the table to stand proxy for the issue you're trying to talk about.   Place a glass of water on the table for example. As you talk about each area, address the glass as the issue, and not each other. Disassociate from the item you're discussing, and try to address it objectively. When personal feelings and emotions are removed, you can go further with the discussion without attacking each other.

Try this exercise and see if it can help. With practise, you'll find it a great tool to help communicate. Remember you never want to attack an individual you want to go directly to the issue.

Family can be a tremendous blessing and support. It can, however, be an obstacle; especially if you are entering into a relationship, or if you are in a marriage with a spouse who was coddled and pampered far too long in life. You know: they have parents, or a parent, who treats them like they're 10, when they are 20, or 30, or more—that mother who just can't let her baby boy grow up, or the dad that can't see his daughter as anything other than his little girl.

It's great that parents want the best for their children, but there comes a time when the umbilical cord needs to be cut.

This is one of those areas where you need to sit down and form clear boundaries and decide how things will be moving forward. Don't accept the behaviour and let it work itself out; be determined to have those boundaries. Use the water glass and talk it through.

Another area to talk about is the idea of having children. Some people have no desire to have children; they want a spouse or partner but don't want children of their own. For others the thought of having a family with children of their own is a life passion; they can't wait to marry and have children. This may not be an obvious area to discuss but you need to know two things here. One, how many children do you want and what are your desires. Two, what about the person you are looking to get into a relationship with or are in a relationship with, what are their thoughts about having children.

If the two of you are seeing things differently you may want to reconsider the relationship. You don't want to continue building the relationship on the hope that the other will change their mind. By doing this you could be setting yourself up for disappointment.

Family is very important. If we have a good strong family we want to continue that relationship with them and we want to reproduce that in our own lives. As well, if we didn't have the happiest or the best family structure in the world as we grew up, we recognize the value and importance of having that and want to work hard to create that for ourselves and the one we are in a long-term relationship with. There are links to resources to help build and maintain good families. Be sure to check out my website and see if there are some articles that may help you at www.YourRelationshipRescueCoach.com. And keep in mind that I also coach parents to help with family struggles.

What "F" word do you think we'll talk about next...

Jim Hetherington

Thoughts

4

Friendships

There are a number of areas to talk about in friendships. Let's start with being friends with our partner. As partners, we need to support, encourage, and defend one another. Often times, we think about the romance in a relationship, but we forget about the friendship.

Webster's Dictionary defines friends as someone in terms of affection and regard for another, who is neither relative nor lover, someone who freely supports and helps out of good will.

Let's take a deeper look at Webster's definition. Remember when you met the person you are now married to, or perhaps in a long-term relationship with? Remember how you would do just about anything for one another: you would bring them gifts or treats; you'd sit and talk at length about everything; you would do what the other wanted to do, just to be polite. Like Webster's definition, we had regard for the other person; we treated them with respect, and we just wanted to get to know them more.

We would spend time getting to know each other's likes and dislikes, our passions and desires, and our future goals, plans, and ideas. This would fill hours of conversation, and hours of walking, as we got to know each other—as friends.

As we got to know each other, respect and confidence would build between us. We would begin to see ourselves as a team, and we would start to picture ourselves working together and building a life together. There is something to be said about getting to know one another as friends first. There's something respectful that happens in that transition. When we meet someone, and they begin to unfold who they really are to us, there's something exciting about that. It's during that time of friendship that we can look at each other and begin to envision ourselves working and walking together.

Time and effort was given to truly understand what the other person was saying. We would listen with great interest in what the other had to say. And slowly, over time, we became that person's number one fan; we found ourselves rooting for them and cheering them on. We wanted each other to be successful; we wanted the best for each other.

I spent over 23 years working with youth and young adults. I have mentored and encouraged hundreds of students over the years. And I always encouraged them to learn how to be friends first with the opposite sex. There needed to be a deep respect for one another without having any sexual interactions. The need to learn how to be friends runs deep. Value and respect for each other runs a lot deeper when we recognize the person first, and not somebody we can just get something from. I witnessed many students, who were shy and quiet, form into wonderful young men and women, because they learned how to respect themselves and the people around them.

Today, more than ever, I see young men and women disrespecting one another. Neither sex seems to care about the other, or what they want. They only care about what they can get and what they can have. Everybody wants what they want, when they want it, and that is usually *now*. People can be very selfish in friendships by wanting only what they want, and by not caring about the other person's needs or feelings. Don't get caught in this trap of only being in a friendship for what you can get out of it, and contributing little.

There's a fine line between friendship and romance. And it's difficult for many to keep those boundaries clear. For many, the boundary lines don't even exist. We're living in a time when everything seems to be swirled together. There's no real respect for one another. We only value people for whatever we can get out of the relationship. It's very self-serving.

I think it's important for young men and women today to learn these boundaries and keep them clear, to know who they are as an individual and what their value is as a person. If a young man or young woman knows what their values are, they can keep clear boundaries in their life. As they keep those boundaries, they would keep themselves out of situations that may compromise them.

If you are in a relationship or a marriage right now, and you haven't learned how to be friends first, I think this would be a good place to start. Take time now to reinvest in one another. Take time now to start taking those long walks or having those long talks. Reintroduce yourself to one another. Every day, or every week, set time aside to go for walks, and begin to cultivate the art of conversation. Start getting to know each other all over again. Learn what it's like to just listen to the other person express everything that they want to. Don't listen to give advice— don't listen to just give a response—listen to hear. And as you listen to one another, you will begin to hear the dreams come out, and the hopes and the aspirations.

This could be a new beginning for many couples. This could be the reinvention of the relationship all over again, getting back to the simple things: talking, listening, and dreaming together.

After all, this is the point behind the writing of this book: to introduce people to the "F" words that will help form values and help a person know who they are and what they believe in, and what they want in a partner.

If your relationship started at a sexual level first, this might be a great exercise for you to do. Often times, when couples meet, and it's simply a sexual attraction, they don't really get to know each other. Allowing yourself to step back and to get to know each other would be a fantastic thing.

One of the benefits of becoming friends is that we can pick up on the things that really build our partner up. We pick up on the things that emotionally, mentally, and physically charge them and really speak to their hearts. As we get to know each other and learn what these things are, we can begin to charge up our partner so that they're healthy, strong, and balanced.

It could be simple things, like writing a note or a card for the other person, or making their favorite meal, or perhaps serving breakfast in bed, and of course, flowers and chocolates. We can begin to learn what the other person's love language is. Their love language is simply   demonstrating that they are loved and valued in a way that speaks to their heart.

My wife doesn't need a lot of encouraging words, and doesn't need a lot of attention; she is probably one of the most laid-back people I know. But she does love flowers. She doesn't need them often, but she does love to receive them once in awhile. And I've learned, over the years, that she especially loves to have them sent to her work on her birthday. There's something that makes her feel special when a bouquet of flowers shows up in public where everybody can see. That fills her heart emotionally more than anything else.

It's our responsibility to learn what it is that makes our partner feel loved and appreciated, and to try to do that as often as we can.

There are a couple of reasons why I wanted to talk about boundaries and love language.

There is a great need to have good clear boundaries in our lives as we enter into a relationship. Men and women both need to have a clear sense of who we are, and to respect ourselves and the people around us.

When we're in a relationship or marriage, the need to have clear boundaries is very important. We need to settle in our mind that the person we're in the relationship with is the only one for us. We need to settle in our mind that we're going to respect and honor and care for that person, no matter what. It's easy for men and women to allow their eyes to wander. It's also easy for them to allow their thoughts to wander if they get angry or disappointed with their spouse or partner. For this reason, we need to discipline ourselves to always keep the boundaries clear with people outside of our marriage.

Too often, we hear about office romances. Or, today, we hear more about internet affairs. It's so easy to think that the grass is greener on the other side. If we have a disagreement, or we're disappointed at home, or we're not getting the sex or the attention that we want, it's easy to allow ourselves to gravitate towards someone who pays attention to us and gives us what we think we need. However, if we have strong boundaries, and maintain the friendship in our marriage or relationship, we will keep ourselves from going over the fence.

That's also the reason why we want to keep the emotional levels full in each other's hearts. If we look after each other emotionally, and make sure that each other is cared for physically, the desire to wander becomes less. I think there's a balance between disciplining ourselves and being cared for emotionally and physically. We need to take care of ourselves, and discipline ourselves constantly. And we need to take care of each other's emotional and physical needs.

Another area that needs to be disciplined is how we interact with the opposite sex, or the same sex. Lines can be crossed innocently, or unknowingly, by our body language and gestures to one another. In the workplace, or at social events, careful attention should be given to how we act and interact with others, if we're married or in a long-term relationship. Some personalities are very flirtatious and playful. They may think it's innocent and that nothing is meant by their gestures, but it can sometimes be misunderstood by others, especially if that person has a low emotional tank. If they are not being filled emotionally by someone close to them in a significant relationship, flirtatious or fun-loving gestures can be misunderstood easily.

This is especially important for married people and those in long-term relationships. Our hearts need to be guarded so that we don't give ourselves over, and allow ourselves to be filled emotionally by someone else. Emotional affairs can easily and quickly turn into romantic affairs. It's very important that we are careful who we are friends with and how we interact.

I don't think it's wise for a man, for example, if he is married, to have a best friend or a close friend that is a woman. It's too easy for the lines to be crossed in that kind of relationship. I think it's wonderful if couples are the best of friends and they can all communicate together, but for a married man, I don't think it's wise to have a woman as a best friend or close friend.

This is a conversation I think most couples should have at the beginning of their relationship. There needs to be clear understanding of what the boundaries are going to be in friendships and relationships, especially those outside of the marriage. There are enough challenges for couples to stay together, happily and long-term; we don't need any extra interference. As we are getting to know each other, this topic should be discussed so that there is clear understanding as your relationship develops.

It doesn't do anyone any good to get into a long-term relationship, or even be married, and then have discussions about who you can be friends with and who you can't. This discussion should happen long before the problem could even exist.

One other thing I would say about this is, if you are married, or in a long-term relationship, and you are attracted to one of your partner's friends, you should do one of two things: either tell your partner that you have these feelings and that you find it challenge to be around that friend or stay away from them all together. There's no sense tempting fate or trying to fight it, because the outcome may be disastrous—or at least get a close friend that you can talk to and have them keep you accountable.

All of us had friends before we got into a long-term relationship or before we got married. Some of those friendships are deep and long and personal. Some people are still best friends with kids they grew up with and went to school with. For others, they may have long-term friendships with people from their sports teams or other clubs that they were part of while growing up. Then, we have friends that we've met through college or work, or from the neighborhoods that we live in now.

All these friendships that we have influence us in different ways. We invest in each of these friendships differently. Some of these friendships are casual. We simply say hi and goodbye, and we're just polite and talk about the weather and the sports, and that kind of thing. We don't really spend a whole lot of time with them, but they're still friends. With other friendships, however, we have a long history together. There may be many traditions and events that we go to annually. There are the other friendships that are really dear and close to our hearts. These friends are the ones that we hold the closest. We share our deepest thoughts and ideas and concerns, and we really value one another.

If we look at these relationships, we'll notice that they influence us in different ways. I know, when I was younger, some of the guys and I hung out, and all we did was party; that's all we had in common. We liked each other and cared for each other, but we cared more about just going out and having fun. When I got into a serious relationship and then got married, I had to look at and evaluate those relationships. I had to look at how they were going to continue to influence me now that I was married and trying to start a new life. And each of us needs to do the same thing. We need to examine our friendships, and we need to examine how they influence our life. Moving forward in a long-term relationship or marriage, we need to evaluate how we're going to integrate these friendships into our marriage, and look at how they will influence the new life we want to have with our partner.

I think it's a great value for couples to sit down and talk about these friendships. I'm not saying that we should dictate to each other who we can hang around with and who we can't, but I think we need to look at how our outside friendships are going to affect our long-term relationship or marriage. This takes great maturity. It takes great maturity on both sides—to be able to look at your friendships rationally, and evaluate them and decide whether they are really going to be a positive or negative influence moving forward. I think this would eliminate a lot of stress and arguments in relationships, if we would take the time to seriously look at them and evaluate accordingly.

As we have an open and honest approach to our friendships, and evaluate how they can, and will, influence us moving forward, we set ourselves up perfectly for what we will talk about in the next chapter.

You'll find out next what it takes to have a strong _____ together.

Thoughts

5

Future

It's not unusual for us to enter into a relationship, a marriage, or even a friendship, and become discouraged or disillusioned. These feelings don't make it necessarily wrong, but those thoughts may come to us.

I can remember, as a young man, probably five or six years into my marriage, having feelings of disappointment. I was working hard at a job I didn't really like, just trying to make ends meet. I was taking some university courses part-time. My wife and I had our two children then, having gone through three miscarriages during these years, and I started to feel down about my ability to provide, what my future looked like, and how I was really going to make it. I was unhappy with my relationship with my wife. I didn't think she was supportive. I didn't think she was loving me the way I expected or wanted to be loved—the typical guy stuff. I wanted to just work, go to school, and have my wife do everything else: raising the kids and keeping the home, as well as fulfilling my sexual needs.

It was a time where I felt like giving up and walking away. I wanted to just go off into the sunset and not return. In fact, I clearly remember that it was a suicidal situation, not caring whether I lived or not. It was just a completely depressive time.

Here I was with a terrific wife, two beautiful children, and a job to provide for all our needs (even though I didn't like it); and I was studying to further myself and was serving in my community with youth and young adults. But I was at the end. I was so discouraged, and I felt hopeless about my future.

I went for a drive, as I often did, to contemplate and decide what I would do. My drive took me to one of my favourite conservation areas outside of the town where I was living. I got out to go for a walk and sat at the waters edge of the lake there. Thoughts began to stir in my mind, and the endless tasks of home life weighed on my mind as well. There was the inability to believe that I would ever finish school or amount to much more. The thought came to just go in the water and float until I sank. But I was too strong of a swimmer to allow that, so I decided I would just walk— and keep walking, and not return— just leave my vehicle there and go off into the sunset and not return.

Walking down a pathway that took me further and further from my original seat at the lake, the despair became heavier and heavier. Thoughts of my wife and children circled my mind, and the nagging thoughts of my work and school zig-zagged back and forth in my head with each stride. Then I came to a spot in the path that was all sandy. An entire stretch went on for quite a distance with no soil, only soft sand, and it was the width of the path from one side to the other. The thoughts got heavier and heavier, and the walk became more arduous as it became slippery. I wasn't gaining any ground, and suddenly I was aware that I was walking in the same spot, not moving forward at all. After what seemed like minutes, I stopped trying to proceed forward and fell to my knees. I couldn't even do this right. I couldn't run away or get away from my problems. I couldn't even walk off into the sunset, never to return.

It was there that I cried out, and said, "Alright, I give up." There, in that moment, the cloud of despair lifted, and I came to my senses and went back to my place at the lakeside. I had a heart- to-heart talk with God that day, and I committed to growing and serving in a new way: to my family, my work, and my future.

One of the top ten reasons that couples give up on their marriage, and separate, is being unprepared. Unprepared! If we were more prepared, we would set ourselves up for success.

Life can get hard. Life can be tough and relentless with it's demands and requests of us. Sometimes life can throw us curve balls, and that can throw us off course, but sometimes the choices and decisions we make, or don't make, can have the same effect. In order to succeed in anything, we must plan. Would you agree that in order to succeed we must make a plan and then execute that plan?

Let's say we want to have a party. First, we would think about what we want to celebrate: what's the party for? Next, we would decide how many people we want to invite, and then make our list of who we want there. Then, we either send out invitations or call them up and ask if they can come. Before we send out the invites or make the calls, the decision needs to be made regarding the day, the time, and the location. Is it going to be at home, or are we going to need a hall, or a bigger venue? Then food, drinks, decorations, and so on. The point is that if we don't plan what we want, it won't happen the way we want it to.

Our relationships and marriages are the same way. We will have better success if we decide what we want, how we want it, and what it will look like. Too often, people just fall for the first person that comes along and bats their eyes at them. Or we're at a low point in our life, and someone comes along and makes us laugh or feel good, and we give ourselves completely to them.

Don't get me wrong; sometimes instant attractions do work, but the odds aren't that favorable that this kind of beginning to a long-term relationship will last. About 41% of marriages in Canada will end in divorce, with 50% of these divorces happening in the first 10 years; most commonly, between the fourth and eight years. So, many of the divorces are happening to young people in their twenties. And 16% of these divorces will happen after 25 years of marriage. Fifty per cent of marriages will end in the United States, with Belgium having the highest rate, at 70%, and Chile the lowest, at 3%.

The top ten reasons for divorce are infidelity, money, lack of communication, constant arguing, weight gain, unrealistic expectations, lack of intimacy, lack of equality, not being prepared, and abuse. Each of these topics are going to be discussed in these chapters, but it is worth some time right now to look at each of these briefly, and then look closer at them as we go along.

For more about these reasons, go to my website, at www.yourrelationshiprescuecoach.com.

Infidelity (which will be discussed in the *Faithfulness* chapter) is one of the big ones. Today, there doesn't seem to be a strong line between the bedroom at home and wandering anywhere—whether it's a bar, an office, or someone else's bedroom. Absolute faithfulness to one another is paramount. More than ever, there needs to be stronger lines drawn where we will not cross over—especially for men! With the availability of pornography on internet and TV, and in books and magazines, there is a lure, constantly trying to draw us away. And the truth is that this is an addiction that many don't even try to avoid but blindly walk into.

Money will be talked about in the *Finance* chapter; but for now, let's think about our approach to money. These days, money, or the access we have to it, comes right to our homes, in the mailbox or in our in-box. We're constantly being offered credit cards and lines of credit, for which we no longer need to be qualified to have them. We just get a card, and off we go, racking up debt as we spend, spend, spend. Without sitting down as a couple and deciding how we are going to spend, we can get into a lot of trouble quickly.

In the chapter on Frustration, we will look at the need for communication and expressing how we feel. I shared my struggle of the despair I felt early in my marriage, which is something I now see could have been avoided if only I was more willing to talk. Somehow we think we will offend the other if we share how we feel, and therefore, we don't. We need to have an understanding before we get married, that we will, and can, always talk about what is going on, and be honest. This is very challenging for men, and we'll talk deeper on this in this chapter.

Arguing is one of the areas that will happen. We're bound to have disagreements that can be resolved by talking them through. Constant arguing comes from areas of deep seated resentment or frustration that is not being discussed. Men call it nagging, and women say it's just asking, but either way, there are areas that somehow are not being expressed and received in a way that is getting through to our partner; and, therefore, the arguing goes around and around.

An important topic that will be discussed in the *Feasting* chapter is that of eating and drinking habits, and body image. Our bodies are going to change. Some of us, with the genetics we've been given, may not look the same when we are older as we did in our twenties—something for us all to keep in mind. That person we are marrying today may not have the same shapely physique down the road. But one thing we can always do is watch how we take care of ourselves, and try to always look our best. If we don't care about how we look, then we send a message to our partner that they aren't important either. Why? Because they value you, and want you to value yourself as well.

Here's a good one: unrealistic expectations. We put them on ourselves and we put them on others. There needs to be realistic expectations placed on ourselves and our relationship. Don't try to impress others by being something you know you're not, and that you know your partner can't be either. Look for this topic in the *Flexible* chapter.

Intimacy comes in many forms: sexual (physical), emotional, spiritual, and mental. There are so many ways to express intimacy, and more often than not, we don't show it very well, if at all. Men look for sexual intimacy, while women tend to want the physical in the way of holding, snuggling, and so on. There needs to be a deeper understanding and awareness of the need for intimacy, and we'll get into this later when we talk about *Frisky*.

Today, many of the roles in the home are shared, like the role of providing. With many homes having two income earners, there is a more compelling need to share the duties around the house. The mindsets today are divided. Both of us may want the dual income, but one of the spouses may want to keep the home structure old school—where the wife does more of the child care and home duties, and the husband comes home from work and retreats to the family room, garage, or home office to do nothing. Strong dialogue needs to happen here so that both sides can feel equally respected and have equality in the responsibility of home life. More on this as we look at *Family*.

Not being prepared is one of the reasons for divorce, and the main reason for this book and you reading it. It's my desire to help educate and open dialogue, and help inform and challenge you so that you are more prepared. As a licensed wedding officiant, when I share some of these principles with couples when we first meet to discuss their wedding, they reply, "We're good." Far too often, people enter into marriage blindly and are not prepared. Just because we watch movies with lots of stunt car driving scenes, that doesn't make us a stunt driver or an expert at all. The same holds true for marriage. Just because we have watched all the classic wedding movies, and we've seen a dozen happy endings, it doesn't prepare us for marriage. It doesn't come natural for all of us. We need to go through some exercises to help form ideas and concepts around marriage, and then be prepared to practice and work hard. As I shared earlier, of the marriages that end in divorce 50% of those marriages end between years 6-10, showing that we may need to be better prepared.

Sadly, the topic of abuse is on the list of reasons for divorce. It can come out of so many areas: infidelity, communication, drug or alcohol abuse, and so many other reasons—not excuses, just reasons. Sadder still is that we can be prepared for everything in our marriage, and this can raise its ugly head for many unforeseen reasons. We'll discuss further in the *Flexibility* and other chapters.

In order to have a strong future together, there needs to be strong planning. There's an expression that says, "We don't plan to fail; we fail to plan." Couples don't get together with the intentions of failing; they fail because they don't make the time to plan and work on the future plan together. They just wait and see how things unfold, and hope for the best. When it doesn't unfold in the way they want, they throw in the towel and move on. A large percentage of marriages end in separation between years six and ten. That means that young couples in their twenties are getting separated; many for the reason of not planning and not having things work out the way they hoped they would. And couples with twenty-five years and more are separating for the same reason. The future wasn't what they wanted, and they've had enough.

Simple solution: Have a future plan, adjust it as you go, and grow into it.

This can be a part of your vision statement. Look at the long-term picture, and ask where you both want to be at the end, when you retire or slow down. What's the common goals the two of you share? Then, backtrack the vision, and start to plan the steps you need to take in order to achieve the goal. If it's a house on the beach, start to dream what the place will look like, where it will be, and what you will do there. When you can both begin to see the dream, and you have a plan to get there, it becomes a team effort, and you work and strive together. If you don't know where you want to have this house, then at least agree on the outcome, and work for the details as you go.

It's important to set smaller *stage* goals as you go. Stage goals are the goals you set for different stages in your lives together. When you're a young couple, stage goals may be buying a camper or trailer, so that you can enjoy some family retreats and vacations. My wife and I used to get season passes to conservation areas, and go hiking, fishing, picnicking, and camping throughout the year. We started to plan trips as the kids got older, and we traveled the country and saw many places together. Later we bought a large fifth wheel camper and kept it at a park were we would go often as a family and as a couple together.

When the kids are older and going off to college and university, you need to maintain an identity as a family and as a couple. Once the kids have graduated and have started their careers, they will move out. Yes, children will move out and move on to build their own lives! It may seem like that day will never come, but I'm telling you that it's true and that you need to be ready for it. Too many marriages fall apart after the kids move on because there wasn't any planning, and the parents lost their identity as a couple and don't know what to do when the nest is empty.

When I first started to drive, I got my motorcycle license and rode bike before I got my regular license. I enjoyed riding, but when I got married, I hung the helmet up and drove cars and minivans until the kids grew up. Around the time that my son had moved out to start a new career in another city, and my daughter was halfway through college, I began to get the bug to ride again. It was interesting for me that as I was contemplating getting a motorcycle again, my wife brought it up in a conversation. She asked if I had thought about riding again, and I said that I had. We began to discuss getting a bike and beginning to do some weekend rides and get- a-ways. We both began to look for an older bike that we could get, just to see if we both wanted to get into riding. We purchased a touring bike and started to get out as often as we could—and we both loved it. It wasn't too long after that, that we traded up to a newer and bigger bike, and started to go on even longer rides, sometimes for a week or two at a time.

For you, it can be anything: taking trips together, building your dream home or cottage, getting a sports car, or whatever you want to do together. The point is, my wife and I recognized that as the kids moved on to start new lives and careers, we needed to start doing something new together. We needed to rebuild our connection as a couple, and start to do things together that we were passionate about. We were passionate about our kids; we spent our lives investing in them to see them succeed, and now it was time to rekindle the romance from our youth and carry on with our vision and purpose. There was an awareness in us both that we needed to adjust and refocus on the future vision, and step into this new stage.

And that's really what it is. Your life, as a couple, is a long sequence of stages. We get introduced to each other, then we grow in love and get married. We have a family, raise them, and see them move out and start their own lives. Then we pick up the romance, and grow and mature together. Each stage has tremendous rewards, but we need to plan each stage to make the most of it and reduce the risk of failure.

Which gives us a perfect segway into the next chapter, because you need strong discipline in this area for these and other dreams to come true.

Thoughts

6

Finances

For most of us, our approach to money comes from how we were raised. Right or wrong, our mindsets were set when we were younger, on our approach to money.

We may have been raised in a home where parents were always spending money and giving things to us. We may have been given an allowance, or maybe we received money when we needed it. Either way, we may have thought that there was a money tree in the backyard that just gave endless amounts of money. For many of us, we weren't instructed how to discipline ourselves with money, or how to budget money; we would just spend it, and that's all we witnessed in our family—just spending and more spending.

For others, we may have had parents that were very strict with money. They were very frugal, or we may call them cheap, and they watched every penny, every cent, that they spent. They would make their own things and try to make things last as long as they possibly could, and simply did not waste.

Or we may have been raised in a family where clearly there was large amounts of money. One or both of our parents may have been very successful, and so purchasing things wasn't a problem. This also can lead to a mindset of thinking that everything comes very easily. If there were always plenty of things to go around as we got older, we would expect the same thing to happen.

As we got older, we may have resented the way we were raised. We may have resented our parents being so cheap or frugal. As we got older and got money, we just wanted to spend it. We would go crazy with the freedom to do what we wanted. We may just model the same things that our parents did, if they were spenders. We may think that it's just a normal thing to get lots of credit to have more things, or buy more things, and keep that cycle going.

Regardless of how we were raised and what approach or value was placed on money, we all have to take the responsibility and decide what our approach will be. As adults, when we start to work and build our careers, we need to be mindful of how we spend and what we spend our money on. In the world today, it is so easy to get credit cards and lines of credit; so, we don't have to stay within the limits of what we make—we can just get extended credit and buy more.

This can be extremely dangerous. If we don't have the discipline to live within our means, we can find ourselves sinking in a sea of debt. It's one thing to do this on our own, but as we get in a relationship, it is a dangerous habit to bring into that relationship, or even into marriage.

And what about the image someone like that is presenting to the other person? A person could be deep in debt but come across as being successful. Because they're well-dressed, they drive a nice car, and always have money to go out and do things, that person may appear to be successful. It could be very misleading for others around them. And someone who is interested in getting into a long-term relationship with this person may not necessarily see the habits that go on behind the scenes. So, I think there are a few things that we need to do to prepare ourselves and to form good disciplines with money—and to also be able to recognize what's going on around us.

Let's start with ourselves. Each person should have a budget. If we know exactly how much we make each week or each month, we need to make it our ambition to live within that amount of money. Even if it means sacrificing, or doing without certain things, we need to be real to ourselves and learn to live within our limits. We are only fooling ourselves by taking on extra credit to buy things, and we are only sending out a false image as well.

So often, I've heard people say that budgets are so restricting. It's quite the opposite. Budgets are actually freeing. The freedom comes by knowing exactly what you have, what it's going to be spent on, and what's left over. Then you know whether you can afford to buy a certain item, because you have budgeted for it, and you have put money aside. If we live off the balance of our bank account, we can get into trouble quickly. For example, if we had $5,000 in a bank account, and we were out shopping and a great deal on something we wanted came up, we could look at our bank account and say, "I've got $5,000 that I can use to do this." Let's say it's a new TV with a great sound system, and it's only $3,000, plus tax. We look at our bank account; there's $5,000, so we reason that we can afford to buy it. Then, next week comes along; it's the end of the month, and our mortgage or rent is due. Or the car payment is due, the taxes are due, and our insurance is due. All these things would have been paid for with that $5,000, but we don't have it because we lived off the balance of our bank account. If, on the other hand, we had a budget, it would be easy for us to determine what could be spent, and how.

It's far better to look at a large ticket item, like a stereo or television, and decide how much it's going to be, and how much we want to spend, and start putting that money aside until it's available. Then there's no question; we are dictating where the money is going. We're dictating how our money is going to be spent. We are not allowing our money to tell us what we're doing; we're telling it what it's going to do. And that's the direction we need to go with our finances. There's an old expression: the tail is wagging the dog. We need to get it working the right way. We want the dog wagging its own tail. In this analogy, our bank accounts are the dog, and the tail wagging is the spending. We need to dictate how the spending is going to happen, so that it happens naturally and within our limits.

If we don't determine where our money is going to be spent, and if we don't assign something to it, something will assign itself automatically.

Let's say we found $500. We could look at that, and say, "Terrific, I can do whatever I want." And if we went through the next day—or two weeks, or whatever amount of time—eventually, that money would be gone. And then, if I asked you what you spent that $500 on, you probably couldn't tell me. You would have to think long and hard on what you did with that $500; because you would take it and just spend it a little here and a little there, until it was all gone.

On the other hand, if we took that same $500 and decided right there what we were going to do with it, and we wrote it down on a piece of paper, we would know exactly where the money was going. And that's where it would go. There would be no question and no thinking; we would know how that money was spent. And the truth is, we have greater satisfaction in ourselves, knowing that it was applied to something that it was assigned to, rather than just guessing at what we've done with it.

That's the power of having a budget. We know exactly where our money is; we know exactly how it's going to be spent, and we know that everything in our budget is taken care of. We can give ourselves extra categories to take care of unexpected things. There is so much value in having a budget, and so much *Freedom* as well.

In the workshops that I hold, we go a lot deeper in this area of *Finance*. Much more time and detail are given on how to create a budget, the benefits of a budget, and how to work within a budget. We talk about how to balance check books so that we can keep track of our money and know exactly what we have all the time. There's much skill and discipline that's needed to deal with our finances, and that's what we go into in the workshops. Go to my book website to find out more, or to get a free budget sheet that you can download, at www.increasethe love.com.

The skills and the discipline to work with money, and to handle money, are not taught in many families today. Most of us are raised not knowing how to do simple things with our finances—for example, balancing a check book, or even creating a budget like we've been talking about. We simply go along as children, and our parents take care of things, and we don't think anything about it.

For me and my wife, it was a whole new experience for us when we got married. All of a sudden, we're buying groceries, paying utilities, paying rent, and taking care of a car, and it was a real juggling act learning how to manage money. And that's really what it is: managing. And just like a good manager directs employees so that they get the most production out of them in a day, that's how we need to approach our finances. To manage that money, direct it where it should go, to make the most out of it.

One of the things I see a lot of today is couples getting married, or moving in together, and wanting to have everything all at once. They want the new car; the new house, furnished with all the nice furnishings; and all the extras, like large, flat screen TVs, and wonderful surround systems. And today, more than ever, it's easier to get all those things. With two people working, there's a greater chance to borrow the money that's needed to have all these things at once.

So, there is no longer the need to plan and save and work towards things—we can get it instantly. The cost of that, however, is sometimes the high interest rates the credit cards have, and then we find ourselves just working to maintain the bill payments so that we can live in those nice surroundings.

There's something to be said, however, with starting in humble beginnings. I remember when my wife and I first got married, and we lived in a one-bedroom apartment. It was fun because it was ours: it was our own space, our own place, and we both enjoyed it. When we had our first child, we simply applied for a bigger apartment in the same building. We packed up and literally moved right across the hall. There, we set up our first home with our first child, and it was great. Eventually, we worked towards moving into a house, and then we bought that house from the landlord and called it our own. And there, we lived for over 30 years, where we raised our family and then continued to live and enjoy it ourselves.

Over the years, we did renovations, built things, bought new things, and eventually made that house a home. It was filled with different collectibles that we gathered over the years. It was the home to many pieces of furniture from both sides of our families, which have great meaning to us; not to mention the memories and the moments that we shared with family and friends. And those things, you can't buy. Just because a home is nicely furnished and is big and new and comfortable, doesn't make it a home.

There is an old expression: home is where the heart is. And that's so true. It's the memories. It's the time that it takes to develop those memories, that truly make it a home. We need to get back to the basics of just being content with little, as we grow and develop.

We'll talk a little bit later in our chapter on *Frustrations,* how we can reduce some of the tensions that come in relationships, especially around finances.

It's very important for both sides to be united when it comes to finances. Often, I've heard stories where one or the other partner has secretly been spending money that they've got on their own. They opened up a line of credit, applied for a credit card, or even went as far as putting a second or third mortgage on a house, just to have money to spend. The ramifications are devastating. The other spouse discovers the secret spending that's been going on, and then realizes that neither of them can afford to keep things going.

The magic of compound interest can work for you or against you. When investing, it's a wonderful thing to take a little bit of money, put it away, and watch compound interest increase it. On the other hand, it's complete devastation when we have huge debts, and now we have compound interest accumulating on that debt. Our debts can spiral out of control quickly when we don't manage our money properly.

The object is to be on the same side when it comes to spending and handling money. And I think it's important that both sides are in agreement when it comes to spending larger amounts of money. For my wife and I, we always agreed that if we were going to spend any large amounts of money, that we would discuss it before we made a decision. That amount of money is going to be different from one relationship to another. For some relationships and budgets, spending $100 to $500 can be devastating to the budget if both sides don't agree. However, in other relationships, it may be $3000 to $5,000 that needs to be discussed before anything is spent. So, each couple needs to sit down and discuss this together. You need to both decide what that limit will be, and you both need to honor that and stick with it.

I have found that it has saved me from making some terrible decisions. For example, there was one time when my wife and I were considering to buy a condo in Florida. We had discussed this a few times and, to be honest, I was more interested in doing it than my wife was. But she went along with it, and we looked at various properties and considered putting an offer in on one of the condos. As I said, I was keener on this than she was. And I remember her saying to me, "If this is what you want, then you go ahead and do it. That to me wasn't 100% agreement. But I narrowed it down to the one that I wanted to put an offer in on, and I was going to make the move, but I stopped. Because I didn't have full agreement with my wife, I waited for a couple of days, and then I waited a couple more. And during those few days that I stopped to consider and discuss it more with her, a couple of things happened. Suddenly, our economy, in Canada, took a little bit of a turn, and our dollar dropped; and that meant that the US dollar rose. When we calculated how much the condo and closing fees, as well as other fees, were going to be in US dollars, we realized that it was going to be a terrible increase for us. So, if I would have pushed ahead with my own personal agenda, it could have made it very stressful for the two of us over the course of time—our dollar didn't get better, and the US dollar got stronger, which made things much more expensive.

So, when it comes to making financial decisions, it's always best that you discuss having a limit where you need to bring the other partner in on making that decision. This will bring less stress and less complication to your finances.

Discuss major purchases and how you will buy or finance them. Unity over money and how you treat it as a couple can save you a lot of trouble.

What "F" is next?

Thoughts

7

Frustration

Almost everyone has had times where they have been frustrated with something or someone. In this chapter, we want to talk about how we can eliminate some of our frustrations, and also learn how to control our frustrations.

The word, *frustrate*, according to Webster's Dictionary, is the feeling someone gets from not achieving an object or from not being successful; the feelings of being thwarted or baffled, deprived of what was due, or some fundamental need unsatisfied. This brings with it dissatisfaction, disappointment, and defeat. All these words, all these feelings, make it difficult to finish the task and to feel successful.

We can get frustrated at something for many reasons. For example, we may get frustrated trying to complete a task that we are unqualified or unprepared to do. And sometimes it comes from just not having experience.

For example, many of us have tried to put together unassembled furniture. The pictures in the diagram, or the instructions, make it look so simple and so easy, yet when we try to complete the task, we are ready to pull our hair out and throw the thing out the window. However, once we have completed the task, we understand how it all works, so if we had to do it a second time, it likely wouldn't be nearly as frustrating. Because we now have the experience of having gone through it, we now have reference in our minds, which allows us to complete the task with ease. So many of our frustrations can come simply by not having experience.

The way to help in this instance is to step back and give ourselves permission to learn. Nobody can know everything about everything. We all have to learn new things, and we're all going to come across situations that we have not taken on before. Simply giving ourselves permission to learn, and to take the time to get things done, is a huge step.

Time is the next reason for frustration. With the example of assembling the furniture, we may allow ourselves, say, 30 minutes, to complete the task, only to find out it's going to be 3 hours to complete the task, and that adds to the frustration because we've only allotted so much time.

While running my renovation company, I found that when I was coming to the end of a project, it was always the little things that took the time at the end of the job. And it was at those times when I would often encounter things, which needed to be put together, that I hadn't done before or that were slightly different than the others I had assembled. Shower doors were one of those things. Just when I thought I had them all figured out, an engineer would design a new system, or they would come up with a completely different design that would take me an hour, or more, longer, just to assemble. And, of course, because it's at the end of the job, I have a timeline and a deadline in mind, and this is just adding time that I don't have. Of course, once I completed that task, I would rush to get to the next thing on my list, and— of course—because I'm already frustrated, this task doesn't go well either. I would find that the last day of putting together all the final, simple tasks was often my most frustrating day, simply because I did not give myself enough time to complete things. I knew from experience that I would run into challenges, but I would still try to plow through and get things done quickly.

What I began to do was to give myself two days to do the final things. I moved the deadline up a day in my calendar so that I would have enough time and not get frustrated.

My coach told me, one time, to schedule 1 hour per day just as an extra margin. So, if I was going to schedule an 8-hour day to work, I would figure 7 hours of working, which would give me one extra hour to take care of those things that I couldn't complete as quickly as I thought. Having this extra cushion in my day made it much easier to complete tasks, knowing that I had breathing room. If I got everything done in those 7 hours, then I was ahead of things, and I could prepare for the next day, start the next task or finish early. Either way, it's nice to have that margin so that I wasn't running through the day struggling to get everything done; I had room to adjust.

A good resource I found was in Richard A. Swenson' book called Margin. In it he talks about having margin in our lives to take the pressure off. Margins are the boundaries, or borders that are around the edges of pages in a book. They keep the pages neat and orderly. Without margins the words would crowd the page falling over the edges and sides making everything look disorganized. Our lives he points out can be like that. He compares margins and overload. Overload is anxiety and margin is security. Overload is hurry and margin is calm. Overload is fatigue and margin is energy. By cramming too much into our daily routines and schedules we can actually be causing more harm than good.

By taking a little bit out of each hour and each day we would give ourselves room to breathe and complete tasks with far less effort and stress; thereby reducing frustration.

We have talked about a couple of reasons that can frustrate us. One is not having experience, and two is not giving ourselves enough time. A third reason for getting frustrated with something is simply doing something that we don't want to do.

How many times have you found yourself doing something you just don't want to do? It may be something that isn't in our skill set, yet it has been given to us to do, and we just don't want to do it. Or, in our relationship, being asked by our partner to do something or to go someplace— we just don't want to, yet we do it anyway, and that can frustrate things. I think one of the big things to exercise here is communication.

My wife and I sometimes have different thoughts and approaches as to how we want to do things. I have a schedule in my mind of the things I want to do around the house, for example; but my wife will have a completely different schedule in her mind. Both of us want the same outcome—the tasks done—yet our approach, and the system that we want to use, is different. The frustration comes when I just start to go about the tasks without communicating, and do them the way I want to complete things. And then she might ask me to do something, which I had planned to do later, but I hadn't communicated that with her. I try to do it her way, and in her time, but it adds frustration—because now I'm doing something in a different order than I had already decided. But because I didn't communicate it with her, and just started to do the task because she asked me to, everything gets tense. Now she can sense my resistance, and she starts to get flustered; and because I'm doing something in a way I didn't want to, my blood is starting to boil.

All of this could have been avoided if we simply took 10 minutes, before we started the tasks, to come up with an agreeable order to get things done, and an agreeable timeline. How many times have we thought that the list of things would only take a few hours, so we've gone ahead and made arrangements to meet up with somebody later, only to find that our partner has planned an entire day of getting things done. It adds to the frustration, and now we're trying to rush to get things done, and then, BANG! Everything blows up—all from a lack of communicating each other's expectations.

In work situations, if we simply communicate that we don't have the skill set to comfortably complete a task and ask if there's something else that we could do, it would save a lot of frustration and aggravation. Now, we have to differentiate between reasons and excuses. If someone asks us to do something, and we're not qualified or experienced to do it, that's a reason. If we're just being grumpy, miserable, or lazy, and we don't want to do something, then it's just an excuse.

We need to have an honest look at ourselves and what we are really qualified to do. Sometimes things can be learned rather quickly if we just give ourselves the time and permission to learn how to do them. While some things are simply better off being delegated to someone else that is more qualified or suited to do those things.

Can you see how approaching things this way would save a lot of frustration? By being honest with ourselves and to those around us, we can save so much frustration. Or at least minimize the chance for things causing frustration.

Frustration can cause a ripple effect in our relationships. If we get frustrated with our partner, that frustration can easily grow into anger, and then into resentment, and then can lead to bitterness. Most of us have had experiences where we have said something out of frustration, which we didn't mean. And those words can be very difficult to take back. When something

---

has been spoken, you can't *unspeak* something. Once those words go out of your mouth and into someone's ears, they can't be taken back. We can ask for forgiveness, and we can receive forgiveness, but sometimes the words have done damage that may be hard to repair.

Another thing that can cause frustration is doing something when we know we don't have enough time to do the thing we're trying to squeeze in. Our schedule may be tight, or we're in a hurry, yet we think we have time to do one small thing; and it blows up in our face because there simply wasn't enough time set aside to do things properly.

Be realistic and only do things that you plan to do, or for which you have the proper time scheduled. Remember to keep good margins.

In our marriage relationship, getting frustrated could begin to build a lack of trust or confidence in each other. It can keep us from wanting to do things together in the future, just to avoid frustrating moments, or going through the same experiences. Getting frustrated with one another can keep us from building great memories—because of being frustrated at something and turning against each other.

In our work relationships, it may keep us from advancing in our career. Those in charge, or those who oversee us, may not want to continue to give us new tasks because it just frustrates us, or we say no to them. You become the person that nobody wants to give new things to because of your reactions to those situations. Being willing to take on new things, and giving yourself permission to learn, can greatly help your career or business.

For example, in my early days of my renovation company, I would often find myself getting books or videos, or watching YouTube, to learn how to do a particular task that I've never done before. Then, the next day, when I tried to do that task, I at least had a reference to go by, and I would give myself extra time to learn to do it.

When addressing issues of frustration, there is a need to look at our inner game and our outer game. In order to set ourselves up for success, we need to look at both sides. The inner game is looking at our mindsets: being prepared mentally by looking at or reading material, and also by looking at our own beliefs about ourselves. Sometimes we're defeated before we even start a task because we say we cannot do it. These limiting beliefs will defeat us and frustrate us before we even start. Sometimes we need to have a hard look at these root reasons of why we believe what we believe about ourselves, before we continue.

Also, our mental game is important. If we listen to what others have to say, that can defeat us and frustrate us. If we listen to people say we can't do that, or we're no good at that, this can affect our approach to just about everything. Listening to our own negative thoughts can begin to defeat us and frustrate us. We need to make the shifts in our own thinking: get rid of the negative beliefs and negative affirmations and begin to set our minds straight.

Remember what Henry Ford said: *"If you believe you can or cannot do something, you are right."* In other words, if we believe that we can do a task, we are right; but if we believe in our mind that we cannot do the task, we are also right. Most of the challenge is in our mind. It's in the way we approach a situation or circumstance. We need to decide whether we can or can't, and we need to decide whether this is a reason or an excuse.

The outer game is just as important; this is our environment. If we are trying to complete a task that we've never done before, and we're tripping over materials and tripping over tools, and we just cannot move or work because our space is crowded and untidy, that's not setting us up for success. Time must be taken to organize a space: clean it up; have things that we need, close at hand; and remove other things that are just going to be in our way. Having our environment set up in a way that is spacious, convenient, and comfortable is a far better way to start a task—especially one that we have never done before, or that we're not too confident in doing.

This explains two main reasons for why we get frustrated: by not being prepared mentally and dealing with those mental blocks, and also for not having our environment set up so it's conducive to what we want to do.

 When a couple is first married an important hurdle to get over is that of sharing or merging our time. It's almost impossible for us to maintain our lifestyle and routines that we had when we were single. Once you are together it's important to look at and discuss routines and schedules. And it's certainly unrealistic to believe we can hold on to that same routine once we have children. Children are awesome and have an interesting way of changing your schedule and how we approach time.

A great amount of frustration can enter into our lives if we are trying to maintain the routine and lifestyle of when we were single. Once we enter into a long-term relationship, or get married, life is going to change a little bit, because now we have another person included in our life. We need to make way for new approaches in almost everything that we do. We may be able to keep our morning routine, our eating habits, and some other personal things that we like to keep the same, but other areas of our lives will definitely change.

Our social calendars will need to include not only the things that *we* want to do, or the friends that *we* want to hang out with, but also those of the one who is close to us: our partner. Now that we have them in our lives, we also have to share some time and energy and other resources with them. One hundred per cent of our time is not going to be our own. Many of the things that we now do will include the other person as well.

If we are unwilling to make any of these concessions, it's going to cause major frustrations in our relationship. We cannot forever keep making excuses or reasons for why we don't want to do things with our partner. Eventually, we will have to make those adjustments.

As we talked about earlier, the key to having success here is simply communication. It's communicating with each other by expressing what our expectations are and what boundaries we are willing to move. We all need to have our personal space and personal time, but we also need to incorporate time together, which will mean adjusting our schedules to include not only the things that are important to us and that we want to do, but which are also important to our partner. If we love them and care for them, then we need to share ourselves with them.

It doesn't have to be frustrating. It can be as easy as drawing up a schedule; if, as a couple, you were to sit down on Saturday or Sunday morning, and take a piece of paper, or sit in front of the computer, and write out Sunday through to Saturday. Then, write down different time slots, starting from when you wake up in the morning, and then block out the times that you need to do things through the day. For example, give yourself an hour or two for your morning routine. Make time for praying/ meditating, exercising/stretching, then get yourself ready and off to work. Then, block out the time that you need for work, and then schedule in your supper and your evening routines, breaking it down hour by hour, and do that throughout the week. I think everybody should get into the routine of marking out their week as a schedule, and outline goals for the week. As a couple, you can then begin to cross reference your schedules, and place in them exactly what you need to do, where you need to do it, and at what time. Keep in mind that you want to schedule time daily where you're together, at least for a meal, to talk and to share about your day.

This is a great way to eliminate frustrations in relationships, especially once a couple starts having children and it adds extra stress on the already busy days. Remember that if we don't assign something to the time, something will assign itself automatically. So, take charge of your days, take charge of your week, and schedule all of your activities; and, of course, mark down goals for the week so that you can obtain them.

Doing everyday things—like working and exercising, shopping, raising children, and dealing with family issues—can soon become a source of frustration. If we don't set ourselves up for success in any of these areas, they can quickly become areas where we aren't very successful.

Up to now, I've been using a lot of examples for work and completing tasks. And you might be wondering what they have to do with marriage or relationships. All of these environments can affect our relationships, just the same as they do in work. For example, every couple eventually will try to take on a work project around a home. It won't be too long into any project before the frustrations will begin, because we're going to take on things that are new to us, which we have never done before, and that could be a challenge.

As we enter into a marriage or long-term relationship, we need to not only examine the "F" words that we've been talking about in this book; we need to also examine the things that we are bringing into the marriage or relationship.

Everyone of us has different experiences growing up.

While we are on the topic of getting frustrated, we should

talk about fighting and arguing fairly. We all know that when we get frustrated, tempers seem to rise, and it's easy to say things that we don't want to say, which happens in the heat of frustration.

One thing that we need to remember is that when we are frustrated and our blood pressure is high, it's far too easy to make things bigger than they really are. When someone's frustrated and says something, the other can easily take offense to it, and then, of course, they say something back; then, the other says something back, and before you know it, it's a full-blown war of words.

Taking a step back is a hard thing to do, but when things start to get big or over-inflated, it's a good idea just to step back, take a deep breath, and reflect on the situation.

One thing to remember, ladies, is that men often like to get the best of something, especially if they're being beat. In other words, they don't want to be defeated. If some nuts and bolts won't go together in a new fixture of some sort for example, they're going to want to get the last word by putting them together at all costs, and that's just the way they are designed. You women, on the other hand, for the most part, can be a little bit more reflective and calmer about the situation, and a little more rational. Also, when a man gets frustrated he will likely just grunt and struggle harder to complete the task so as to not be defeated. Women want to talk about it, reflect and discuss what the plan is going to be. Remember the differences between men and women and their approaches to problem-solving, when you're up against something that's just not going right.

When there are big, ongoing issues that are causing the fighting, or arguing, and you need to talk things through, I encourage couples to sit down at a table, preferably across from each other so that they can look into each other's eyes and really hear each other. Then, I suggest that they take an object, and put that object in the middle of the table—it could be a cup, a vase, or a bowl, or a bag of marsh mellows, that could sit on the table between you—which becomes the object you're talking about.

So often, I see that when people try to discuss an issue, they take it personally and can't seem to look at it objectively. By placing an object on the table, it's much easier to view the problem, or situation you want to discuss, more objectively. And when you're talking, don't take things personally and try not to use language that is attacking the other person. You simply want to discuss the situation objectively and refer to that object that's on the table.

By using this object, and referring to it as the problem, you will find it easier to discuss the situation and not take things personally. As soon as your language starts to become more directed to the other person, stop, and simply address the object on the table as the problem. We never want to get into a battle of words or insults when discussing a problem or an issue. Remember that oftentimes the things that we're talking about or arguing about are just objects.

If it happens to be something a little more personal—for example, the way we raise or discipline children—then that's when we need to refer to our mission statement. We talked about this, and this is a good thing for all couples to have as they enter into a long-term relationship or marriage: to have clear values, goals and objectives, which we believe in and stand for, written down so that we can refer to how we want to handle things. This can include, as we mature in our marriages and relationships, children, and the goals to raise them, discipline them, educate them, etc.

Practicing these principles that we've outlined in this chapter will begin to help us to be less frustrated or aggravated in situations. And it also will give us tools to use to help discuss things and to talk them through rationally and productively.

In my training seminars, I use my workbook to look at all these different areas and give couples the opportunity to begin this work so that it becomes clear. This workbook is also a great resource to use along with the book as you're reading. Find out more about it by visiting my website, www.increasethe love.com.

Thoughts

8

Faithfulness

This is a powerful word, and one that we shouldn't have to talk about, but today, more than ever, it's necessary. All kinds of ideas are portrayed throughout media and movies, and even music videos, that suggests that faithfulness is not necessary in relationships. In fact, today, it's almost expected that partners will be unfaithful in some way. Over 60 per cent said they would cheat on a spouse or partner if there was a guarantee they wouldn't get caught. We are given unrealistic expectations, regarding relationships, from social media. Look at the reality shows people view; some are disappointed if the drama they see on TV doesn't follow in their own life.

It's not uncommon to read about unfaithfulness or infidelity throughout history. For almost as long as there's been man and woman, there has been, and will continue to be, sexual tension between the sexes. However, for the past few generations, with the increase of movies and social media, the whole idea of being unfaithful, and having multiple relationships at one time, is portrayed as being both exciting and a desired reality.

Now, more than ever, entire generations are being influenced by music videos, TV shows, and movie characters. The introduction of reality TV has brought with it a twisted glamour that attracts people more and more. Many young people, today, are embracing this reality as their own, and are carrying it into their relationships. They almost expect it to be a part of their lives.

Let's look at the meaning of the word, *faithfulness*. Webster's Dictionary describes it as being steadfast in belief; loyal, accurate, and true to the original; to have trust and confidence; to be with honest intentions; to resolutely stay with a person without waiver.

Let's start with *"to be with honest intentions."*

When we first meet someone and get to know them, we're testing the waters to see if our interests and values line up. We are getting climatized to each other as we get to know each other's personality—the way they think, and how they communicate with us and the world around them.

It's at this point that we're using these "F" words that we are discussing throughout this book. We're looking to see how our faith lines up with theirs; we are observing their approach to finances; and we're finding out their future goals and direction. Over time, we're getting to know their family and friends more, as well as their feasting habits.

Slowly, over time, as we see that our values and our directions lineup, we begin to build confidence in each other. We start to discover the common ground that we have, and we start to connect on a more emotional level. It's at this point that we start the crossover from a friendship to a relationship. We go from *growing in like* to *growing in love*.

I think there's a difference between *falling in love* and *growing in love*. When we fall, there is the image of just dropping uncontrollably. People fall from heights, or people can fall off of a high ledge or cliff. We say things like, "he slipped and fell," or "he took a nasty fall." We wouldn't say "he slipped and grew," or "he took a nasty grow." It just wouldn't make sense. But when we grow into a relationship, there's the idea that we continue to develop, and that we continue to evolve.

If we planted two vines in the same planter box, at first, we would be able to identify the two individual vines. As they grow and develop, the vines would begin to intertwine, and you wouldn't be able to recognize it as two plants; rather, it would begin to look like one. The two vines would begin to use each other for support to grow and to develop, making it even more difficult to identify them individually. It's the same in a relationship. As people get to know each other, they're like those two vines, planted side by side. First, you could tell that they were two plants, but then, eventually, they grew to look like one. Our emotions begin to develop together, and our hearts become like one as well.

With this relationship at this level, there is the unspoken expectation that the two of you will be faithful to each other. Now, I know that there are some progressive couples that are very open in their relationships. And they may discuss right from the beginning that there is freedom to see other people during the relationship. But I wouldn't endorse this or encourage it. Just as in our illustration of the vine, if we were to put two or three other vines in that same planter, it would become very, very confusing. In fact, if you had too many vines in one pot, they would begin to choke each other out at the roots. So, in my view, it's very important that a couple remain faithful to one another, and to one another only.

So, apart from these *progressive* relationships, there is the intention, as couples get to know each other and move into a more serious relationship, of being honest and loyal to each other. The intention is to honor the other person and to speak truth, with no deception. We intend on sharing our true feelings towards one another, and keeping communication open.

We could take that example of the planter with the two vines a little further. Let's consider the planter as being the personal space around our lives together. Treat it like a garden: if you were the only two plants in that garden, you would spend time keeping other plants and weeds out, that would cause any harm. We would be very careful with what we planted around us. We would only allow things that would be healthy for our growth together, to come into that garden. And it's like that in a relationship. We need to be careful of what we allow to come into our lives. We don't want to have unhealthy relationships interfere with ours, and we don't want to invite things into our lives that may be a distraction or may be harmful.

As well, we would do everything in our power to protect each other. We would watch each other's backs, and we would be alert to things that could jeopardize each other.

Can you begin to see how important it is to value each other and care for each other in this way? As two people grow in a relationship together, they need the physical, emotional, and mental support from each other. And if this is our intention from the start, then we need to remain faithful; that is true to this original form.

The Amish have a terrific expression: Choose the one you love, and love the one you chose. Out of the billions of people in the world, we have lots of options and lots of choices. Once we've made that choice, we need to be faithful to that choice, every day, reminding ourselves why we chose the one that we love, and then work hard to make the other person happy that they chose us as well.

Let's talk a little bit about choices.

Choosing someone to be in a relationship with is like being a kid in a candy shop. We have a look around, and there's so many different colors and sizes and flavors, that we don't know what to choose at first. But then, as we begin to examine them, we begin to realize there are certain things that we don't like. There may be certain colors or flavors that we don't like, and we can eliminate those immediately. And then we can examine the other ones and decide according to the colors, flavors, and sizes, which one suits us best. Sometimes, if we don't take our time to really decide which one would be best for us, we can reluctantly choose something, only to regret it later. It just might not be exactly what the label indicated it would be, and that can be disappointing.

In the real world of relationships, it is important for us to know ourselves, and to know the things that we like or dislike as we make our choices. This is why it is important for us to not only examine ourselves and know our own values, but to take time to really examine and know the values of the other person before we move forward into a relationship. Buying the wrong candy and going back and getting something different is a whole lot easier than trading in or trading out of a relationship.

So, men, let's say that you decide that what you like is a tiny woman with blonde hair and blue eyes, and you enter into a relationship with one, then she is your favorite. If it's a taller, robust woman, with auburn hair, then she is your favorite. And, women, if you like tall, dark, muscular men, with brown eyes, then that's your favorite. If it's a shorter man, with no hair and blue eyes, then that's your favorite. Once we enter into a relationship with our favorite choice, that's where eyes should stay.

In short, what I am saying here is, once we know ourselves, and we know what we are attracted to, and we enter into a relationship with that type of person, that's where our attention and our focus should stay—on that person. You chose wisely, and once you've made your choice, be faithful to it.

The problem that some people get into is that they let their mind and imagination wander, even after they've made their choice. We need to exercise self-discipline and self-control in the area of relationships. We can look endlessly and wonder what it could possibly be like with dozens and dozens of people. We can always think that the grass will be greener on the other side of the fence. But if we discipline our mind and thinking, and get back to the place of just caring for the garden we have planted, things would be much better.

Take the time and choose well, and once you've made that choice, be faithful to it.

Things will always happen that may cause us to think, "What if?" Thinking "what if" is no way to go through life. To constantly ask ourselves—what if I made another choice; what if my husband was smarter; what if my wife was in better shape—all these *what ifs* will only cause us to doubt. And where there is doubt, insecurity and uncertainty will follow.

As our relationship develops and our marriage grows, there are going to be disagreements and misunderstandings; that's inevitable. But just because these things come along, that doesn't mean that life as we know it is terrible. And we can't go around looking for emotional support all over the place. I think it's important for men to have some close male friends that they can share with. And I think it is equally as important for women to have other women that they can share with. These are areas where you are safe and can share freely. It's only when a male begins to confide in a female, and a female begins to confide in a male, that trouble could be on the horizon.

Now, I know there are some exceptions. But as a rule, I would never encourage a person in a long-term relationship or marriage to consider confiding their problems with the opposite sex. Far too many affairs have started this way. We've all heard stories, or perhaps know from personal experience, of someone who has shared their deep hurts and regrets with someone of the opposite sex, only to have an emotional, then a physical affair.

And I use the term, *emotional affair*. Many people are guilty of having emotional affairs with others all the time. And they think, because there's nothing physical, that it's completely okay. I don't think it is. In couples' relationships, there needs to be complete loyalty— physically, mentally, and emotionally. If we start to share any of these three things outside of a long-term relationship or marriage, we are robbing ourselves, and our partner, of having 100% of our affection. There is no room in a long-term relationship or marriage to give any of our physical, mental, or emotional energy to anyone of the opposite sex, other than our partner.

This is where faithfulness is demonstrated. We need to support one another fully and completely, 100 percent of the time, with our physical, mental, and emotional strength. That's what builds a strong relationship. That's the foundation on which we build. Greater confidence comes when we share our deepest feelings with one another.

One of the biggest breakthroughs in my marriage came with this revelation. I thought I would be happier if my wife did everything my way. I thought that if she would keep the house cleaner and give me more freedom to do the things that I wanted to do, and also be available for all my sexual needs, that life would be great. I couldn't figure out why she wasn't responsive to my physical needs all the time. It didn't seem to matter what I did or didn't do, nothing would change. Until, one day, I stopped focusing so much on trying to change her, and started just to change myself. I focused my attention on being a better husband, father, and partner. I started to develop my character and my strengths, and I started to work on my weaknesses. Then, an amazing thing happened: my wife became more attracted to me; and suddenly, I felt more fulfilled in all the above mentioned areas.

It's important for us to remain faithful and disciplined in our lives. Don't spend time wondering *what if,* or *if only*, but rather stay focused on the relationship you chose, and be the very best person that you can be in it. Equally as important, I think, is that we have a responsibility to look our best for our partner. Don't *let yourself go*. Often times, after we get into a long-term relationship, we begin to take less care of our physical, mental, and emotional selves. Some think that once they have a partner, they don't have to care for themselves anymore. And that can't be further from the truth. I think we have a responsibility to look our best for ourselves and for our partner. Nobody wants to be accused of the switch and bait. That is, advertising one thing and then switching it for something less or different. We need to put full effort into looking our best and being our best, throughout our relationship and marriage.

My wife, for example, will always put on a little makeup and do her hair, even when we're just sitting around the house on a day off. This is something that she has always liked to do. As she says, "I want to look good for my man." And it goes both ways. Men, take pride in how you look and how you care for yourself. The same way that you tried to show off for your bride when you were younger, you should take that same pride today and show it in the way you care for yourself. We might have a little extra weight around the middle, and we might have a little less hair than we did back in the day, but we can still take pride in what we have. Do your best to eat well, and get rid of those ratty and torn shirts and pants, and look your best.

In doing this, you are expressing to each other that you care. When you try to look your best and do the best with what you have, the message sent is, "I still care about myself, and I still care about you."

You need to ask yourself, "Would I choose me today, to be in a long-term relationship, if I looked like, acted like, or treated people like I do today?" If the answer is no, then we need to ask ourselves why not. And if there are things that we can change that would make it more positive, then we owe it to ourselves to do it.

And that's the other reason to remain faithful. Faithfulness builds over time. Confidence and trust—they all build over time. And that can't be replaced in a single, momentary action of passion with somebody other than our partner. Having sex with someone can happen anywhere, anytime. But true passion, and true intimacy, only happens over a long period of time. This is what is built in a long-term relationship. Over time, through our actions of being faithful, true depth and meaning really happen between two people, and this is hard to replace.

So, remember to remain true to your original form. Remember the original intent that you had when you chose your partner. I have the privilege of performing wedding ceremonies often. And during the ceremonies, I will encourage couples to remember why they said "I do," and to remember why they chose each other. It's remembering why we chose each other that will get us through all of the difficult times. The problem can sometimes be that we just throw our hands up and give up too easily. There's a lot of hard work between the happy pictures that we take with each other. The photos that we see in our scrapbooks are a glimpse of the highlights in our lives. What isn't documented is all the difficult and trying times in between. But it's there that the true intimacy is cultivated. It is there that we grow deep together and demonstrate how we value one another.

This all takes time but is well worth the effort.

If you and your partner struggle in this area, coaching may be of benefit to you. I meet with couples and walk through a five-step model to create a plan that will help them move forward together. If you're interested in learning about individual or group coaching, go to my website, at www.your relationshiprescuecoach.com, and find out how to get your free session, and discover how it can help.

You're going to love this next word!

Thoughts

9

Frisky

If you're wondering why I use the word, *frisky*, for this chapter, I use it because the word itself means to be lively and playful. And in this chapter, I want to talk about the lively, playful, and fun things in marriage. In other words, the intimate and romantic element in this relationship.

If you haven't noticed already, there is a big difference between men and women. I know it's a surprise and a shock, but it is the truth. And I'm not talking just about genetic makeup, or the physical appearances; I'm talking about our attitudes and approaches towards intimacy.

Women, in general, are open with their feelings and emotions, and generally want to talk about most things, or everything. It's important for them to have a good handle on every situation. So, when things don't seem right, they always want to talk about it or discuss it so that they know exactly where things are. And in terms of marriage and long-term relationships, most have given them long hard thought, most of their life. Women, when they're young girls, imagine what it would be like to get married, to have a family, and start a life with someone. A lot of them play dress up and have tea parties, and do all those wonderful things as little girls, all the while preparing for when they get older.

Now, I want to just put a disclaimer in here before we continue. I recognize that girls don't just think about tea parties and all those other things. Many of them are growing up dreaming and fantasizing about being in the corporate world, or having construction careers, and other wonderful things. Please bear with me; I'm just talking generally.

Now, for men, as they are growing up, they aren't giving too much thought to anything at all. They're just winging it, day by day. Thoughts of how to stay out of trouble, and how to get away with as much as possible, rule their minds most of the time while growing up. Many of their thoughts are just on how much they can sleep or play, or how much fun they can have. And again, I recognize that there are many women that would fit into this category also. But remember, I'm just speaking generally.

When a man and a woman get married and enter into a long-term relationship, they're already coming from two sides of the coin. One has thought about it for a long, long time, and the other really hasn't given it too much consideration but knew it would happen someday—because there is one thing that most guys know intuitively: they don't want to be alone.

Even when it comes to intimacy, there's often two different sides of this as well. For most women, they like to cuddle and feel that affection, and to have the affirmation and security that comes from being held. Many of them have grown up being *Daddy's little girl*, and they want to continue to feel that warmth and security. Early in the relationship, there is often a bit more sexual interaction as the two are just getting to know each other. But as time goes on in the relationship, when it's time to go to bed, women would really just love to be cuddled or held, and go to sleep, most of the time.

Now, for the fella, it's a little bit different. Remember, he's growing up not thinking about very much. However, once he hits a certain age in life, women are very much on his mind. The idea of having sexual relationships is something that he is very passionate about. In the early stages of marriage, men just can't get enough sexual interaction. Oh, sure, they don't mind cuddling and being that security, but believe me, their thoughts are going much further than just cuddling. They're thinking, "How can I turn this into having sex?"

When women are lying in bed being held in the arms of her lover, she is thinking that it is a dream come true. Reflecting back on all the fantasies of what marriage would be like, it has finally come true, and here she is with her knight. When a guy goes to bed, his thoughts go more like this: "There is a woman in my bed! This is great! I'm going to have all the sex that I want!"

Two different people, with two different approaches.

There needs to be an understanding from the start of any relationship or marriage. Women, you are never going to convert your man into a best friend, like one of your girlfriends. Yes, he will be your best friend, but it will not look the same as your relationships with your girls.

Girls, you talk about everything. If something is wrong, or you're upset, or you're nervous about something, your first response is to talk about it. Guys aren't like that. When most guys get nervous, or they're thinking about something that may be troubling them, they say nothing. They think and reflect inside. That's the way they deal with it. By you coming at them and asking them to share their feelings, this will only cause them to withdraw more and probably say less. Ask a man what's wrong, and you will usually get short answers: "Nothing," "I don't know," or a grunt.

Men think and contemplate on things. When they get troubled or they get worried, they withdraw and think. Probing and prodding them won't speed up the process; in fact, it will usually make it worse. When they come to the end of thinking, they'll reach out and begin to talk. Once they have time to process and look at the options, they'll begin to reach out and draw close to you, because one thing is for sure: men don't like to be alone for long. They need you, but when something is brewing on the inside, they need to retreat and think. T.D. Jakes refers to it as going into the cave. When a woman has trouble, she wants to go into the village and talk, but when a man has trouble, he wants to go to the cave and think. Trying to pull him out too soon will only drive him further back into the cave. Give him time. He will come around, but the process is different between men and women.

Remember this when you are building your relationship, and you will overcome a huge obstacle. Remembering this will take most couples past a breaking point and to a place where true intimacy can grow.

I could have actually included this topic in the *Frustration* chapter, because it is often a source of frustration for both men and women. Because we come from two different sides of the coin on this, it is often the center of a lot of frustrations and discussions in marriage.

I think men and women need to discuss intimacy in marriage, and keep an open dialogue about it. It's important to talk about this area rather than just avoiding it.

And just as an FYI to all the women out there, it doesn't matter how many layers of clothes you wear to bed, your man is still going to find you sexy.

One thing to keep in mind when talking about this area of intimacy is to be mindful of your partner's history. There's a need to understand how they were brought up and how they were raised. It's necessary to understand their past history and whether there was any abuse or promiscuity when they were younger. Both of these things can leave a person feeling insecure when dealing with intimacy in a relationship. Again, as I said earlier, it's important that we talk about these things and have open dialogue. Intimacy is getting to know one another in a deep way. When we begin our marriage and enter into a long-term relationship, we're partners for life, and we need to know everything about one another.

Self-esteem and self-image can also be some of the baggage that we bring into a relationship. Having low self-esteem or poor self-image can have a life-long effect on you as an individual, but now that you're married, it will affect you both, as a couple. So, the things that you bring into the relationship, all the baggage that you bring in, isn't just yours—it becomes *ours.*

If you can share these things together, and deal with them, that's wonderful. Keep in mind, however, that you may need to get outside help to really deal with these issues. Today, there are so many ways that we can get help: We can talk to religious or spiritual leaders; we can get counseling; and we can get coaching. All of these things are aimed to help us grow, and to deal with past and present issues.

As my wife and I shared our past hurts and wounds, at first it felt a little embarrassing, but over time, as we discussed things, we drew closer together. Mike Myers, in his movie, *The Love Guru,* although it was a bit wacky and crazy, had one or two interesting things to say. The one thing he said, which stuck with me, was taking the word, *intimacy*, and breaking it down to mean, *into me I see.* When we share our past hurts, our true feelings, and things that have wounded us, past and present, that's intimacy: allowing the other to see into you. In intimacy, there grows a deep respect, honor, and love for one another. This can only happen when we share.

Guys, it's not about entering into a marriage just to get all the sex that you want, and to grope your wife whenever you please; it's also about making her feel secure, wanted, and loved, as well as making her feel valued and important. When she walks into the room, you want to make her feel that she's the luckiest woman in the world because she's with you. That's intimacy; that's the foundation of a long-term relationship. When we get to a place like that, and our hearts and emotions connect, the physical will just naturally happen. When a woman doesn't feel she's just an object to be used, but rather a person who is loved, cherished, and valued, that goes farther than anything else.

It's also important to talk about our expectations regarding sex. We talked earlier about setting family goals so that we understand what our expectations are with children, and it's equally as important to talk about what our expectations are with sex.

When a man or woman keep their expectations and what they want in a relationship to themselves, they are robbing their partner of the opportunity to know them. When we keep things in our own minds, they can make lots of sense to us, and we can dream and fantasize about all kinds of crazy things. It's only as we share them and bring them out into the open, into the light, that the truth can really be understood around what our expectations and motivations are. By keeping them in our minds, we're being selfish; by sharing them with the other person, we're being generous—because it's through sharing that we give the other person permission to enter into our world.

This will also take away the frustration that we will have in this area. When things are out in the open, and we can make a plan and agree on things together, there's less frustration. It's a terrible thing to go to bed, night after night, hoping for intimacy but not receiving it. And it is also a terrible thing to go to bed just hiding from intimacy and trying to avoid it. And both men and women can be guilty of both these things. When we're open and honest, then the truth can come into our relationship, and we can have a healthy, happy, sexual, and intimate life together.

Then there's the area surrounding things that we picked up along our way in life. It may be things that we picked up in movies or in videos, or on social media, which may not really portray true intimacy and sexual relations. We may have received poor information from somebody who perhaps meant well but might have had terrible experiences, and have shared their thoughts and perspectives with you. It's a good thing to really share those thoughts and ideas, and reflect on whether they're right or appropriate.

I heard of an account of a mother who took her daughter aside the night before she was about to be married. She had a heart-to-heart talk with her daughter, telling her what to expect when she gets married. And the advice the mother gave was this: "When you get married tomorrow, your husband is going to want to lay with you and do terrible and nasty things to you, but this is what needs to happen to have a family."

Now, I don't know about you, but I don't think the mother really set the daughter up realistically. It may clearly be her thoughts and ideas about sex, but to set her daughter up in the same way is really unfortunate.

It's necessary for us to really look at our sources, and the motivations of those sources, that we get our information from.

Sharing things will bring balance and clarity to both sides.

We need to know what the other person is thinking. If you're going to be life partners, you need to, and want to, know what the other is thinking.

Sharing your desires with one another is another important

thing to do. Telling each other what you like or don't like will help set good boundaries as you move forward. Neither partner should be forced to do something that they don't want to do. There needs to be mutual respect for one another and each other's bodies. You should only want those things that are appropriate, and that you both feel comfortable with, to be expressed in your relationship.

Plan your times together. This can be helpful for both sides. If you both agree on a time that you're going to be intimate, it gives you both something to look forward to, and it will also help you to plan your time. When we schedule moments of intimacy into our routines, we can do what's necessary throughout the day to make sure our time and energy is freed up for these moments.

For the guy, this will keep him from being forceful or begging through the week. If you have a scheduled time when you're going to be romantic, his focus and energy can be focused on other important things until that moment comes.

That doesn't mean that we wouldn't give ourselves over to spontaneous moments, as these can be some of the most fun and romantic times. One should never feel that her husband will think less of her if she just gives herself over to him spontaneously. I've heard women say that they don't want their husband to think less of them because they give themselves over too often. On the contrary, it will only build the intimacy when we give ourselves over to each other in love. When we plan our times, and give ourselves permission to have spontaneous moments, it will only help both sides.

And, as a side note to the men, when you have planned these moments of intimacy with your partner, don't be all nice up to the moment, and then, afterwards, neglect her and don't pay her any attention. It's important that we follow through, day after day, and be consistent in both our affection towards her and our willingness to help around the home and with the family. You should never make your wife feel less valuable before or after intimacy. She should always feel loved, cherished, and valued.

Make times where you do just cuddle and hold each other. Have times and moments where you just kiss passionately and nothing else. These moments are good for the heart, and it is good to keep the expectation of future moments, and times of intimacy, present.

It's important to remember that you both have a responsibility for each other in the area of sexual intimacy. It's important that both of you share your wants and desires in your relationship, and it's important that you follow through on what was agreed on. I think both partners should want to care for each other in this way, making sure that both feel fulfilled in their relationship all the time.

Too often, I talk with couples or hear stories where the intimacy has been lost, and one partner begins to look outside of the relationship. If more time could be spent knowing each other in a complete and intimate way, perhaps there would be less wandering outside of the home. If the woman feels loved and valued, and the man feels wanted and cared for, both sexually and emotionally, I feel that there would be less infidelity.

Now, I'm not saying that just having sex all the time will solve all these problems, but what I am suggesting is that if we were less selfish and more open in our relationships, perhaps the cheating and the wandering would not happen. As I mentioned earlier, once we get married and we're in a long-term relationship, the person that we chose is the person with whom we should have our soul affection. Discipline and self-control are things that needs to be exercised in our relationships, especially in our sexual relationship.

I'd like to also add a note to men. The drive that we have inside us isn't only to be satisfied sexually. We can take that drive, and harness that energy, and put it to use in so many ways. It can be used to propel us forward in our careers, life planning, and in so many other goals.

Think of all the coaches that have encouraged players not to have sex before a game; especially a playoff game or any other important game. They knew that men can take that sexual drive and harness it to become more aggressive and more determined to succeed. Oftentimes, after they've had sex, the first thing men do is roll over and fall asleep. Or afterwards, they're just so relaxed and weak in the knees that they're not good for too much. On the other hand, before the sexual release, they had the drive and the energy to do just about anything. If your wife said that she would only be intimate if you carried her up three flights of stairs, we would gladly pick her up and carry her up those stairs, because that drive and that passion, and that energy, is so strong.

Napoleon Hill, in his book, *Think and Grow Rich,* has a powerful section where he talks about men using their sexual drive to further themselves. I know, it's hard to imagine that there is anything else we can do with that sexual energy other than just have sex. But my experience, in the more recent years, has shown me that the sexual drive can certainly be harnessed and used creatively as well.

Have fun, be frisky, and frolic! Give each other the space needed, and respect the place where you are both coming from. You have a life to build together; make sure the foundation is good and solid, and build it together.

Which leads us perfectly into the next word...

YourRelationshipRescueCoach.com

Thoughts

10

Forever

Once again, I call on Webster's Dictionary to describe our next "F" word, *Forever*: without a break, or so often as to seem so. It's not so much about duration of time as it is the consistency of being—being in such a state that it feels like there is no break or pause. Putting it into relationship terms then, to be together forever would be consistently sharing and expressing your love and commitment to one another, where there is no break, just constant and continuous affection.

Imagine living with someone, and the entire time you're together, there isn't a break in the way the two of you express how you feel. The way this would happen is having a complete commitment to loving each other, and to focus on that only. There would be no room for any other thought to enter into your mind—only complete and total focus on love, and love only. You would have to hold love in the foreground of your mind and not let any other thought enter. It would take so much focus and strength to hold the thought of love in your mind. Every time something would try to enter, you would have to force it back out.

Let's say that a couple had a spat about something. One of them said something about the other's appearance, and it was taken personally as an attack on them, and that was the start of it. It's quite easy to have this happen, isn't it? Someone turns to us in conversation and says something, and we take it the wrong way and go off on the other person in a rage. Or worse, the person offended says nothing at all, and gives the old silent treatment. How many times have we witnessed that response? When this happens, it's easy to hold on to the offense, and over time, it becomes deep, and the person holding on to the offense can become bitter. That would interrupt the consistency of love being expressed. The only way that two people can stay away from being offended is to be so focused on love that they don't entertain any other thought than love.

It would take tremendous concentration and discipline by both of them. They would need to determine right from the start that neither would focus on anything other than love. As soon as an offensive thought or idea tried to come into their mind, they would have to shut it down immediately. And it would only take a split second for it to happen. We've all been in situations where somebody has said something to us, and in a split second, we needed to decide whether to retaliate with insult or let it go, and respond in love. It takes less energy to respond negatively. It takes no effort on our part to just react and say negative and hurtful things. On the other hand, it takes a whole bunch of energy to hold back and respond in love and grace. Think of a time when someone has done something that we have taken offense to. Now, think of the thought process. They say something, and then the wheels start turning in our minds. We are thinking, *they said this, and I could say this or that*. Then, we start to justify it in our minds but convince ourselves that it is our right to respond negatively. Right? We start with the conversation in our mind. *Well, they did this and this, so I'm perfectly within my rights to say something hurtful to make me feel better about myself.* Then, the choice comes. Do we say the hurtful thing to make us feel good about the situation, or do we let it go and respond in kind?

This is the moment that the *forever* is broken. This is where it becomes strained and stressed.   The moment we entertain any opposing thoughts, our *forever* is threatened.

One of the biggest problems is that in the heat of the moment, we don't care. Sometimes we get so fired up that we don't think clearly. We don't respond—we react.

These are two different things: responding and reacting. For an example, we put our hand on a hot stove, and the immediate reaction is to pull our hand away. We're wired to pull away because of the way our brain has been conditioned. Many of us have had an experience like that in the past, where we were hurt in a situation, and now our brain is taking control and reacting almost instinctively. It may not be a hot stove, but there has been something in our lives that has caused us to react when a similar situation comes up. It's our brain's natural way to protect us. Or when we were young, somebody or some situation may have scared us. Now, if we are scared, we want to react by hiding or running away. Even if we sense something may be coming, we start to feel ourselves wanting to react the same way we did when we were young.

In the case of the hot stove, we want the brain to kick in and compel us to remove our hand. When we are frightened by something or someone, we need to first assess whether there is an imminent danger or not before we react. This is where we want to respond, and a response takes some thinking. It takes some analysis and some processing of the facts before a decision is made. For example, let's say that you are working in an office, and you've gathered in the lunch room with some coworkers. As you are all gathered and talking, someone accidently drops something, and it makes a loud crash as it hits the floor. Without thinking and giving some thought to what it could be, let's say you just react and run because it scared you, and you're aren't sure if it's a bomb or if the floor is about to give out. You'd look pretty silly, wouldn't you? If you just reacted out of the fight or flight theory, without giving it any thought, you could be looked at as cowardly, or as a *fraidy cat.* By us reacting without giving any thought to things, it could turn out to be critical for us. The ability to respond to situations is important to our safety and to the outcome, and the same can be said of our relationships, marriage and otherwise. The discipline of thinking through things before we say or do anything is huge. Many disputes and misunderstandings could be avoided if we exercised this discipline.

Let's take another situation, this time at home. Suppose you and your partner are doing dishes together. You're both working away in the kitchen and chatting as you go, and suddenly, a cup slips out of your hand as you're drying it, and it smashes to the ground. A reaction would be saying something like, "You dummy, what did you do that for? You're so clumsy; you're so careless." That would be a reaction that could hurt the other person deeply, and it could start a big argument. On the other hand, if we asked if the person was okay, and if we assessed the situation first, that's a response. No one gets insulted, nobody gets lashed out at; there is just a simple dialogue and you move on—even if it's your favourite cup in the whole world. You look at the important things first. No one was hurt, and you can replace things one way or another.

Many of life's challenges can be handled differently, and the outcomes can be tremendously different if we would take time to think first and then respond. When we react to a situation, we are reacting from an already heightened sense of urgency.

We are coming from a place of high alert and are making a decision out of that heightened state. We need to take a step back, take a deep breath, and evaluate things. And this can take as little as a few seconds; it doesn't have to take hours or days to readjust. Some things and situations may take more time than others, but generally, a few seconds of effort is required to make it happen.

It's the effort that is the real challenge. It's so much easier to react on the spot and just let into the person about the situation. It takes no real energy or discipline. And that's why people turn to it first—because it's easier. In order to break through and respond, we need to apply self- discipline. That's right, the terrible "D" word: DISCIPLINE.

Discipline is given such a bad rap. It's always used in a negative. We may have flashbacks of childhood, when we may have been disciplined for doing something wrong, and so, now, we want to stay away from that word. Discipline has become a swear word in the minds of countless people. But it's the very act of not being disciplined that causes many of the problems we have. If I discipline myself, that means to hold myself accountable. I hold myself to a higher standard. And that is the thing that is needed to live out our *forevers.*

This act is what starts to bring us closer together. There's an old saying that states opposites attract, and many of us may be in a relationship where that is true. In fact, most relationships have this in common. There is something amazing and predictable in human nature, and that is that for some crazy reason, we like people that are opposite. When it comes to regular relationships/friendships, we like people that have the same interests. We choose to hang around like-minded people; ones with whom we have a common interest, like sports or a hobby, or work, or something. For the most part, we want to be surrounded by like-minded people, and we take comfort when there are people around us that share our ideals and values.

In romantic relationships, we want someone with whom we share common interests, but there is also something that attracts someone to a person who is the complete opposite.

In many relationships, you'll see an introvert with an extrovert; someone shy with someone more outgoing; an adventurous person, with a timid, reserved person; and so on. There is sometimes something attractive to a woman, for example, to be in a relationship with the *bad boy*—that rebel-hearted person who lives on the edge. People that are shy may gravitate to someone that is outgoing. There may be a desire in us to be like them; we can live vicariously through them, and we want to be around them. You may have even caught yourself thinking, or saying out loud, "What is she doing with a guy like that," or, "How did a guy like that get a girl like her?" Opposing personality traits balance one another out; we can keep each other grounded.

My wife and I for example are very much opposite. When we first met she would have a plain hamburger, I wanted everything on it. When we sit outside she wants to sit in the sun and I want the shade. She liked her steak cooked well done and I like it medium rare. One of our friends noticed how opposite we were; he said my wife is black and I'm white. This friend took a picture of us one afternoon and the light coming in through the window, you guessed it, made my wife dark from the shadow and me brilliant white from the light. He screamed with excitement, " See I told you, you are black and he is white!" Over the years of being married however, we have come to compliment each other wonderfully.

For some marriages or long-term relationships, this can present a problem. Because the personalities are so opposite, and their positions and views are so far apart, it can be hard for them to come to an agreement on many of life's decisions or issues. Picture it like an old weighing scale, the kind where you put weights on one side and then balance it up with a product or something. When the scale is balanced in the middle, it is equal, and the values on both sides are the same. It's like that in a relationship. When a couple starts out together, they can be vastly different in the balance on the scale of common interests or common ground and agreement. The goal is to come closer and closer together in the middle, so that they balance one another.

We've all seen couples like that. They compliment each other perfectly. It's almost poetic to watch how they share and interact together. I believe that for all marriages to function well, they need to get to that place, and they can get there if they are each committed to making that happen. As I said earlier, some personalities are easier to mesh. Some take a lot of effort and focus for that to happen. But it can, if we are willing to do a few things.

First, is to think of the other person first. If we were to spend more time wanting to help the other to succeed every day, we could get to that place. To put another person's need first is counterintuitive. It doesn't come naturally for most. Great effort and thought has to happen in order for this to take place. Remember how we talked about reacting versus responding? This principle applies here. In order for us to put our partner first, we will need to step back and consciously resist the impulse to put ourselves first. But as we do, it will become easier and easier with each opportunity. It will come more natural. As we do this more , guess what? The other person will notice what's going on, and they, in turn, will start to do the same thing. There will be less and less tension around the issues where you are putting them first, and the journey to the middle of the scale spectrum will have begun.

Second, we need to believe that we don't have to be right all the time. Ouch! This may be hard for some personality types, but there is great benefit to the relationship if we just choose the battles. Choose the areas in which we do stand up and say, "No, you're wrong," and then allow others to just go. For example, let's say you're setting the table. One partner insists that you put the plates and napkins around the table first, and then follow up by going around and placing the silverware out next. While the other may say, "No, I'm putting the silverware all in place first, and then the plates and glasses. The outcome is going to be the same, and in this instance, the process just doesn't matter. Just do whatever way is going to have the least amount of resistance, regardless whose way you follow. I figure if it's not life and death, then it really doesn't matter.

My son worked with me in my renovation company years ago. He was just out of high school and wasn't sure what he wanted to do, so I suggested he work for me until he figured that out. At first, he followed my direction because he really didn't know what he was doing. Quickly, however, he picked up things and was starting to take some initiative on how things were done. We started to have lengthy discussions on the process of things, and he was starting to have strong opinions about things. I would point out that it should be done in such and such a way, and he would argue that it should be done in a different way. Not wanting to discourage him, I found myself biting my tongue and allowed him to take some of the direction, and I only stepped in if it was a safety issue or a cost-effective issue. We developed a great working relationship, and he grew and became a very gifted leader in his field. I think, however, that if I had squashed his initiative, it may have turned out differently.

Many marriage and long-term relationships are the same way. Many a person has found themselves squashed under the rule of a dictator-type partner, and were not able to grow to their fullest potential. And isn't that what we really want for each other? Isn't that the kind of environment we would want for each other? But too often, things are ruined, simply because we want to win all the battles. We have this need to be on top and in control all the time. A successful relationship pushes one another up, not down. We want to elevate the other person, not deflate them.

Third, ask for our partner's advice or ideas. I was terrible at this when I was first married. I had to be the man and show my wife how much I knew. I had to show her how competent her man was, and do everything myself and my way. Only as I relaxed my role, and swallowed my male pride a bit, did I see how incredibly important and valuable it was to ask for my wife's advice. And you know what? She constantly amazed me with some of the ideas and approaches she had. And it built her confidence up and made her more willing to put forth ideas and suggestions moving forward. She knew she wasn't going to be slammed for sharing her ideas and thoughts. And I'll tell you something else: I really began to value her take on different people we met, and who we were going to potentially do business with. She had this innate ability to pick up on subtle things in a person's personality, and she was often right on. Listen to each other, and encourage one another to share thoughts, ideas, and insights.

After all, that's the value in having opposite personalities. They see things in completely different ways from us, and that gives us an advantage. Together, we can come at a situation from two different angles. Like they say, two heads are better than one! So, take advantage of having the opposite view, and put it to work. It's the idea of synergy. One plus one doesn't equal two; it equals three, five, or ten. The combined energy that happens when a couple puts their heads together, to work on a task or issue, is multiplied. Your thoughts and their thoughts combine and produce thoughts and ideas you never would think of on your own.

That's the power of a couple working together to find solutions to financial goals and other goals, rather than just trying to win the argument and push their own idea.

Forever is a long time and it is possible to achieve. It takes a lot of hard work and discipline and you will find over time that as you grow in love your interests, thoughts and passions will come closer and closer together as you go. Once again I would suggest taking the Kolbe test and use it as a tool to help you see how each other operates. Once you see how each other is wired you can make the adjustments needed that will strengthen your communication and give you better insight as you navigate life together toward you forever.

For the link to the Kolbe website and other resources be sure to go to my website www.YourRelationshipRescueCoach.com.

The next "F" word can be both good and bad.

Thoughts

11

Feasting

Let's talk a little bit about eating and drinking. This isn't an area of life we often talk about, or even examine, but I feel it's worth a look.

When we meet someone, it's usually in a social environment. It could be at work, school, the gym, or some other place. If it doesn't involve food or drink, it will eventually. And when we meet for a meal or to have some drinks, we don't consider the amount that's being consumed.

It's not uncommon for any of us, when we go out for a meal, to splurge or treat ourselves. We'll have the extra-large portion of steak; we'll add the baked potato with lots of sour cream or butter, and we'll have some deep-fried foods for appetizers or for our main courses, and then, of course, there's desserts. We'll say things like, "Well, I don't normally do this," or "Just this one time, I'll get this," and we don't think anything of the other person's language or what they eat or consume.

It's not uncommon for a couple to open a bottle of wine and consume the whole bottle during the course of a meal. And we may have a pre-dinner drink and not think anything of it. We can justify it or write it off as just being a treat, because it's a special occasion.

And then, one date leads to another, and to another, and each date may involve another bottle of wine or two, a couple of beers, or a couple of post-drinks, or whatever the case would be. And even if we meet privately at one or the other person's home, we would offer them a drink, and have some snacks, with little thought to what we're consuming.

As time goes on, we may notice little subtle things with regards to diet or drinking. We may notice that the person gets the extra-large fries and the extra-large soda, with every hamburger that they have. Then, maybe, extra salt or butter, or whatever the case would be, on food, but we don't think anything of it—because we're socializing.

And it's the same with drinking. It's socially acceptable to sit down and offer a drink or two, and as the conversation continues, the drinks can continue to be poured. We may notice when we come to this person's house that if they have other friends over, socializing might always be around drinks. Or when we meet them for lunch or at some other time of the day, we notice that their breath smells of alcohol, but we don't think anything of it.

Eating disorders are a little bit harder to recognize. If a person is rather obese, or even just somewhat overweight, we may look at it and think it's cute, it's nice, they're big-boned, or whatever the case may be. Other eating disorders, like bulimia or anorexia, can be even harder to see. These disorders are typically hidden really well. And we may think that the person is just extra-thin. But if we sit and think of the amount of food that's consumed, and the times that the food is consumed, we may begin to see some of the signs. But again, sometimes love can be blinding. Infatuation can be extremely blinding. We're more focused on the person's appearance, their personality, their wittiness, and just the sheer enjoyment of their company.

These are all distractions that may keep us from really seeing the true habits that are going on in a person's life.

Now, I have no problem with eating good food, and enjoying drinks with that food. I am a foodie, and I love good food. And I enjoy having a good glass of wine or a nice craft beer with my food. So, I'm not talking just about eating or drinking; I'm talking about the patterns around eating and drinking: the patterns we develop around eating and drinking become habits. And habits can become addictions, and can be very unhealthy if we don't keep them in check.

For example, when I'm sometimes on the road and very busy with my schedule, I can begin to just buy food that's quick, simple, and easy. And that can easily become a habit. I may just pull into a drive-thru food place to buy anything quick and easy to get me going again. And, even with drinking, it's easy for me, sometimes, when I'm stressed, or again, working too hard, to come home and justify having an extra glass of wine or an extra beer with a meal, just to relax. After a few days of this, however, I need to really check my schedule, and my eating and drinking habits, to get them back in line. It would be far too easy just to grab the quickest meal and chase it down with any drink. But as I said, this routine could become a habit.

These habits can easily become an addiction and can grow out of control. These are the things that I think we need to recognize in ourselves, and in the person that we are wanting to have a relationship with. Are we really looking at our long-term relationship when it comes to eating and drinking? It's wonderful to go out and enjoy times together, where we treat ourselves and have special meals on special occasions. But if that becomes our normal habit, it can grow out of control rapidly.

We need to examine our own lives and our own habits when it comes to eating and drinking. We need to determine, ourselves, what we are going to do, what our limits are going to be, and how we're going to treat our body. We need to remember that we're not drinking and eating just for today; we are eating and drinking for 10 years and 20 years down the road. We must stop and look at how we're eating and what we're drinking, and consider the long-term effects. Consider where our eating habits are going to lead us.

Today, more than ever, it is easier to know exactly what it is we are consuming. We can calculate what the effects are going to be long term. We have more awareness of the damage that too much sugar can do to our bodies. We know what the effects of having too much salt or eating too much white flour can have on our bodies. Even restaurants have the calories, the fats, the proteins, and all the nutrients that are in the foods, listed so that we know exactly what we're eating and drinking. Even in corner stores, bags of chips, cans of pop, and everything else, has an ingredient label to tell us what's in there and how much we're consuming. We are educated and informed, more than any other time, on exactly what the effects are and what we are consuming. It comes down to our choices. Once again, remember that we are not eating just for today—we are eating for 10 years and 20 years from today— because what we consume today will have effects, positively or negatively, down the road. Somebody once said that if they knew they were going to live so long, they would have taken better care of themselves.

With today's medicines and technology, many of us could well live into our 80s, 90s, and beyond. Start taking better care of yourself—now!

Now, you may be thinking it's not our place to judge. And you're right. Everybody can eat and drink what they want. It's not about forcing them to do something; it's deciding whether you want to be connected to that person. I've talked to people that got married to a person they knew had a drinking problem. They thought it would be okay if they married this person and that there would be no issues. But this person ended up being abused by their husband— physically, mentally, and emotionally. It got to the point where it was life-threatening, and she had to leave to save herself. That's the dangers of drinking, and we haven't even talked about drugs or other substances. All these things need to be considered before entering into a relationship. Before we are emotionally attached or romantically attached, we need to look at the signs, if there are some, and decide how they line up with our values and the direction we are going.

It is much easier to untangle things early in a friendship than it is to call things off once we're in a deep relationship, or even married. Once we are married and have children, it becomes far more complex and dangerous.

Think about your own circle of friends. You may have examples around you; examples of where a relationship or marriage has gone wrong because of eating disorders, drinking habits, or substance abuse. Have a look at the outcome of some of those lives and the family situations, and decide for yourself if you really want to go through that, or if it is worth evaluating things early. Decide what the deal-breaker is. Decide what values you have in these areas.

It doesn't have to be a heavy intervention. It doesn't have to be you saying that they shouldn't do this and they must do that. Just simply talk about it, because the truth is that the other person may be doing these things because you're doing them. They might think that this is what she wants to do, or this is what he wants to do, so we'll just do it. And together, you could be forming habits in an unhealthy and unnatural way, just out of courtesy.

I found that people who don't really have problems will talk about things easily. Sometimes those people that do have issues will try to dismiss it by playing it down, saying it's not a big deal, or they may become really irrational or defensive about it. That could be a warning sign that something really is wrong. If you calmly say, "Hey, I'd like to do something else other than going out to the bar, or going out for some drinks," or, "Let's just have water with our meal tonight." On the other hand, if it's met with strong objection, or even anger, then you know something may be wrong. Only someone with a drinking problem would really get angry about not indulging for an evening.

Brian Tracy said, *"Bad habits are easy to form but hard to live with, and good habits are hard to form but easy to live with."* This is true about any area of our lives. But it's especially true about drinking and eating habits. Good habits are much easier to handle in the long run. As I mentioned earlier, we are not eating and drinking just for today; we are drinking and eating for 10 years or 20 years from now. Our bodies aren't designed to handle long-term abuse. There will be consequences in the long term, based on the way we treat our bodies today.

There's another side to eating and drinking habits, and that's to do with our mentality. I can remember running into a couple of guys that I went to high school with. They were partiers and only cared about what was going on today, and not about tomorrow. When I ran into them, it was like they were still in high school; they had that same mentality. All they cared about was drinking and living for the day. I'm all for being carefree and enjoying life, but if 30 or 40 years down the road, you haven't matured or grown any, that's a tough place. Think about being with a person like that long term. Would you want to spend 20 or 30 years of your life married to someone, or in a deep relationship with someone, who doesn't want to mature or grow up? I don't think so. So, the habits that we form when we are younger may stay with us throughout our entire adult life. We all know of people who can't hold a job and can't be responsible for anything because of drinking or substance habits.

When we can control our eating and drinking habits, it shows a lot of self-discipline, and the self-discipline we have for our own life will carry over into how we treat others. A person that can control their tongue, control their attitude, and has great control over how and what they eat or drink, will often care for others around them in a very healthy way. The ability to say no to having one more, or just that little extra, shows great discipline and respect.

And that's really what it comes down to: respecting ourselves. To have such a good self image of who we are and where we want to go is an incredible place to be. Deciding ahead of time what is valuable, what we will accept in our life, and the way we are going to be treated, all says so much about how we respect ourselves. And just the same as the person who shows great self-discipline, the person who respects themselves will often respect others as well.

Part of self-control, or self-discipline, is knowing our own personal limits. We need to know our bodies and how much we can consume and how much we can eat. I always tell people that you don't want to drink until "stupid" wakes up. We all have seen people who have drank too much; all of a sudden, a completely different person emerges. This person may be over-emotional, extra-aggressive, argumentative, or even extra-loving—either way, something happens when too much alcohol is consumed. So, we need to know what our limit is, and decide what that's going to be—because we don't want to drink until "stupid" wakes up. Remember as well, if someone was to drink so much that they loose control and don't remember things, that means that someone else has control over them and the situation. No body should be in a situation where someone else can have control over them because they've consumed too much.

For me, I will only have two drinks in a five or six-hour window. And it's not that the third one wakes "stupid" up; I just find my brain is cloudy and I'm too relaxed, and I don't like the effect that alcohol has on my thinking. So, I may have a second glass of wine with a meal, but I will not have a third one. Decide where your boundaries are. Know what you will accept and what you will not accept, especially when it comes to the company that you keep. Nobody wants to be that person who has to babysit "stupid" once it's awakened. I enjoy good food. And I especially enjoy the way particular wines, beers, and liquors taste with food. Having a really good dish and then pairing it with an incredible wine is just an amazing experience to me. It takes the experience of eating foods to a whole new level. The wines and beers enhance the flavors, and it works marvellously together.

If I abused my drinking, and I couldn't discipline myself or my drinking, I would miss out on all of those experiences. I know of a man who is an amazing cook. His knowledge of food and spices and flavors is incredible; and he can create dishes like nobody else. However, he has a drinking problem, and had to lay alcohol down. He doesn't touch a drop. So, now he has to live vicariously through everybody that experiences the food he creates and the drinks that he suggests to have with the food.

By disciplining ourselves, we can continue to enjoy the flavors and the experiences that we have with alcohol. I encourage you to have a sobering look at your drinking, and how much you consume, and adjust things and put limits where needed.

That brings us to the area of food. This is another area in our lives where we can form some unhealthy habits, even addictions. Because so much of our interaction with people is around food, it's so acceptable to eat, and eat, and eat some more. It's one of those things that we seldom talk about until it's too late.

It would be much easier for us to discipline ourselves as we go, rather than allowing our diets and our eating habits to get out of control.

I discovered, when I was younger, that I'm hypoglycemic (that's where your sugar levels can spike and then go low leaving you feeling lethargic). I had to make major adjustments in my diet, and that was a challenge. It took me months to get my diet under control and to get my sugars where they should be. Now, I regularly adjust my diet to keep everything under control. From my experience, I have found it much easier to make small adjustments as I go, so that I can keep my eating habits in order.

It can be a challenge to keep a balance in our diets, because everything tastes so good— especially the things that aren't good for us—they taste the best! I think there are three things that will be helpful for us to eliminate the foods that we shouldn't eat, or at least eat them in moderation. First, we need to exercise great self-control. Secondly, we need to have someone that we are accountable to, and that we will listen to. Share your struggles with a coach, or a friend or family member, and let them work with you. And thirdly, we need to set ourselves up for success. Eliminate all tempting foods from your house or work place. Don't even have things anywhere near that will cause you to fall.

Let's have a look at each point.

Self control is one of those things we think we can do, but most of us don't exercise good self-control, and we sometimes despise the thought. It's easy to fool ourselves into thinking that we have things under control. But once we finish eating that fourth donut, we know that we're just fooling ourselves. Next, of course, we get discouraged, and then we want to eat more, and that exacerbates the problem. Learning how to say no is vital to success. However, if you can't go it alone, then go to the next stage; get a coach, have an accountability partner.

I'm not talking about taking an extra chocolate chip cookie when they're warm out of the oven, but rather pulling into the drive-thru and buying two hamburgers at a fast food restaurant to eat on your way home after work. We're talking about sitting down and finding it necessary to eat the whole large bag of potato chips, rather than just having a small amount.

We need to ask ourselves why we find ourselves eating or even drinking the way that we do. When we get stressed or upset, or hurt or offended, we need to ask ourselves why we turn to food or to drink. If we can understand what drives us to food, or what drives us to drink extra, then we can deal with those problems, and perhaps control it a little bit better.

This is sometimes challenging for people to do on their own. I'm one of those people who could open a bag of chips, put a small amount in a small bowl, and eat only that portion; I could put the rest away and be fine with that. Others, on the other hand, find it impossible once they know that bag is open—they eat until they're throwing away an empty bag. If we're having challenges in this area of disciplining ourselves and controlling ourselves around food, or even drink, then we need to have people that will keep us accountable.

That's the next stage: accountability.

It may be necessary to share with a close friend or a family member exactly what our struggles are. And we need to commit to those people—make a plan and share our desire—and then allow them to keep us accountable. Regularly, we need to meet with that person to share our successes and our failures, so that we can work on the problem.

It may even be a benefit to have a coach. As a coach, I set up programs with my clients to help them succeed, with a 5-step model. I first clarify their vision and what their goal and outcome is. Second, I strategize an action plan with them; third, if necessary, we upgrade skills, and we educate them in the area that they're struggling with, to help them get over things. Fourth, we optimize the environment, as I mentioned earlier, by eliminating all the stuff that's tempting, and we create a good environment. Finally, the 5th step, we learn how to master our psychology. We work on mindsets and the shifts that need to happen in order for us to be successful.

All these areas are designed in my coaching to help people become successful.

I hope you can begin to see why it is necessary to have a look at our own eating and drinking habits, and to look at the eating and drinking habits of those we care about. It's not about judging; it's about looking at the reality of their actions towards food and drink. And being observant, we can see if there are issues or problems that need to be dealt with. This applies to our own life, and it applies to the people around us. We need to examine our habits all the time, and decide if there are areas that need to be adjusted, or corrected or changed. Another good discipline is to not drink for a week or a month every so often. This helps us to see if it is a problem and it is also good for our bodies to rest. With food, remove one or two things from your diet and constantly adjust it to become a more balanced and healthier eater.

If you're in a long-term relationship or marriage and drinking and eating habits are getting out of control sit down and discuss it. Be open and non-judgmental in your approach. Make settle suggestions to correct the behaviours. Start cooking healthier and balanced meals, eliminating unhealthy snacks. If you have a purpose statement pull it out and talk about how things are working. If however, the habit has become an addiction and if there is abuse or threats, get outside help. Don't stay in an unhealthy or unsafe environment get help. Don't be afraid to reach out. You can even reach out to me by email and I may be able to suggest some resource or next steps. My email again is jim@YourRelationshipRescueCoach.com.

By looking at our own habits, and looking at the habits of our partner, we can move forward and encourage and support each other and together we can work on a strong relationship.

One more "F" word to go!

Thoughts

12

Flexible

By definition, the word, *flexible*, means to be open to influence; to be responsive to changing conditions; capable of being modified; pliable.

As children, we were very flexible. Just sit and watch a child take their foot and stick their big toe in their mouth and chew on it. Or watch the way they bend and contort, and get themselves into all kinds of positions that, as older adults, just make us cringe in pain. Even mentally, children are very flexible. If you tell most children that they can't do this or they have to do that, or we're going here or going there, they're easy going, and they just say okay, and away they go.

As we grow older, we get set in our ways. There are ways we want to do things; we get set in the ways that we want to have things done, and we become less flexible—some of us even to the point of being very rigid. For some, the very thought of having to give into somebody else's way is very foreign. We feel like we're being robbed or violated, because we have to give up what we want, for someone else. I think the person who came up with the expression, "my way or the highway," was a very inflexible person.

In life, I think it is very important to stay flexible, especially in the area of relationships. If we are not flexible, and we are not willing to adjust our attitudes or our way of doing things, it's going to be very challenging in most relationships. Let's face it: things do come up, things do change, life happens, and we do need to adjust and move forward. We need to learn how to curb our disappointments and to not take things personally; because, as I just said, sometimes life happens.

Too often, you see men, for example, come into a relationship, and they have expectations of what their wife or girlfriend should do. There's the stereotypical approach to a relationship, where some men expect the cooking, the cleaning, and the laundry to be done by the woman. Or you may have a woman that enters into a relationship and expects that the man will do everything for her: wait on her hand and foot, shower her with gifts and presents, and all those things. When two people enter a relationship with this approach, there can often be great conflict if neither one is willing to be flexible on their position, or flexible in their attitude towards the relationship—the battle is on.

Tension can happen in a marriage because the man will want to put his foot down and demand things be done a certain way, and the woman is going to want things her way, and to be showered with gifts and presents, etc.

On the other hand, if we approach relationships and marriages with a flexible attitude, it gives us room to grow together. We come into the relationship with a give and take attitude, rather than a take, take, take attitude.

Being flexible is bending, moving, and shaping to your surroundings. It's adjusting to circumstances and going with the flow. Being inflexible is wanting our environment to adapt and shape to us, being unwilling to move. There are many things that we need to be flexible about, like being flexible in our thoughts. It's fine to make plans and have thoughts of what you would like to see done, but if things don't work out the way you want them to, then you need to remember that being flexible is very important.

We need to be flexible in our relationships, in friendships, and in our marriage. As the old expression goes, there's more than one way to skin a cat. It's not the prettiest thought or analogy, but the idea is that there isn't just one way to do something all the time. Sometimes there is; other times, doing something the way a friend or partner wants to do it is going to work out just as well. So, being flexible and experiencing things in a new way is a good thing.

I like routines. I like to know what I'm doing, and I like to schedule my days and my time. But I need to give myself a little bit of time in my schedule so that I can be flexible. I've started to add extra time when I want to do a project or go someplace, just in case something happens; then I can be flexible in what I'm doing.

Having to change my routines and the way I have to do things is challenging. Once a schedule is set, or I have established a routine, it is hard, and sometimes frustrating, to make any change. It's a mindset, and once I make the shift mentally, it's easier to go with the flow. I've learned to be more flexible and less rigid, and it makes the shift easier.

In our relationships and marriages, we need to constantly be willing to change and adapt. This is particularly true for young couples. When we first get together or first get married, life and routine can be easy to manage. As we add children to the mix, however, things will most definitely change. This is the thing that we need to be prepared for. Sometimes little ones just don't get our schedules or our routines, or the things that we want to do.

If we are a person who is flexible and adapts easily, things can go much smoother.

One example I can think of was the very first time my wife and I, and our two young children, 9 and 12 years of age at the time, went to Guatemala to help a missionary couple. People asked us what we would be doing and what we expected. We replied that we would do anything we could do to help the couple, and we really had no expectations. At the same time we went, there was a young couple that had just graduated college and got married, and they were going to be helping the same couple in Guatemala. It wasn't very long into the trip that we got to know the attitude and the expectations of this young couple. They thought it was going to be easy and that it was going to be just like living at home. Their expectation was that they wouldn't have to do very much work, and that they would just be able to relax and enjoy living in an exotic area.

They soon discovered that there were many chores that had to be done: things needed to be repaired in the mission house, and there was always something that needed attention. They started to get frustrated with each other and with the whole system. Because they could no longer sleep till 10 in the morning, and do nothing all day long, they started to get upset.

On the other hand, my wife and myself, and our two children, had a tremendous time because we were flexible and had no expectation on our time there. We were simply there to serve, and went with the flow. If we had to go into town—which, by the way, was a very bumpy, long, slow ride—we were more than happy to go, to help get materials or whatever we needed to complete a task.

Being flexible can be the difference of having an enjoyable time or a disappointing time.

We need to be careful here, though. When we first get

together, or get married, each other is our only real priority. Other than the two of you, your needs and wants, there's not much else that you need to worry about. You have each other's 100% attention and affection. Then, children come along, and the attention and the affection gets divided. It needs to go much further and in different directions. The problem is that one or the other of the partners could feel left out. This is especially true for men—probably more so than for women. It's usually during this time that men feel their physical needs aren't being met. The woman is just thinking of raising and caring for the child, and just trying to survive, often not really thinking about the physical needs of anybody else.

I'm not trying to be stereotypical here, as I realize that many men share in the responsibility of raising the children. However, I will suggest that sometimes we can get so focused on the new routine that one or the other may feel that their physical needs are not being met. These are times where couples need to work extra hard to remember why they're together, to remember why they are in love, and why they said yes to each other. Discipline is needed to continue to work on the romance, and to continue to be flexible with one another.

One of the things that I encourage couples to do when I'm coaching them is to have a purpose statement. In the purpose statement, I get them to write out the things that are valuable to them as a couple: to consider what they stand for, what things are important to them, and what they believe in as a couple. As the relationship matures, they need to revisit the purpose statement to continue to have a fresh vision for who they are and who they are becoming. As the family grows, and the dynamics change, they need to adjust their purpose statement to stay current with their environment.

This is a great tool to come back to and refer to often.

Whenever a couple is trying to decide what to do about something, then they can refer back to this mission statement and see how it fits with their purpose, their value, and the things that are important to them. Both sides can agree to change it, but it's great to have this tool to refer to, and to say that these are the values, this is what we believe in, this is what we stand for, and moving forward, all decisions should fit within that.

I think one of the things that keeps us from being flexible is not being lifelong learners. When we finish college or university, and start working on our careers, often times we just focus on our careers and just go to work. Or we buy a business and we start the business, and that's where all our attention and energy goes. It's easy for us to forget to feed our minds and to grow as an individual. It's easy to put our heads down and just take care of our work responsibilities and our family responsibilities. All of a sudden, one day, we lift up our heads and the children have grown; they have left to go start their own careers, and we suddenly realize that we've had our head down, just working. It's during this time that we can become very inflexible. We can become very rigid in our routines and in our purposes because we aren't feeding ourselves, expanding our minds, or growing.

However, as we continue to challenge ourselves to grow as an individual, and apply and learn new skills, we can stay flexible throughout our lives. We can adapt to change, and we can adapt to new ideas and thoughts, if we continue to challenge ourselves mentally, physically, and spiritually. By the time we are 35 years of age, 90 per cent of the 70,000 thoughts we have each day are automatic. Only ten per cent of what we do each day is new or different. By continuing to grow and learn and challenging ourselves to be flexible and do new things daily we interrupt our brain and force it to do things differently and thereby stay flexible and open.

Welcome new ideas, welcome new friends, and welcome new opportunities to explore and grow, and make new memories. This will help keep us flexible. It does take discipline, and it does take a desire to do this. But the rewards will be amazing. They will outweigh the cost that we have to pay in order to stay flexible. It comes back to what we talked about before: we have a responsibility to become the very best version of us that we can be. By doing this, we help the important people in our lives to become the very best that they can be as well.

As we strive to achieve greatness in our own lives, we will find that we influence the lives of others around us and pull them up as well. We need to have a flexible attitude and a flexible approach in life and relationships; this will make everyone's journey much more enjoyable.

I trust that you found the principles in this book helpful. It is my desire to bring to your attention some areas that can and will help you, moving forward, in your relationships. As a single person, you can use these principles to discover more about who you are as a person. Use these principles to know who you are and what you believe in. Then you can use them to line up a person you may be interested in. By looking to see how they line up with these principles, you can determine if they are a good fit for you.

As a married or engaged couple, you can begin to use these principles to create the values that you both believe in. It's a great tool to use—before, during, and well into a marriage.

Moving forward, please visit my website and check upcoming events, as I hold training seminars and webinars to take people through this material, to help develop better relationships and marriages. I also hold individual, couples, and group coach calls/sessions. You can find out more at www.YourRelationshipRescueCoach.com. And for more information on my other books, please visit www.Increase TheLove.com.

I'm happy that you took the time to read and work through this book, and I wish you a world of happiness in all your relationships.

Thoughts

About the Author

Jim currently lives in Cambridge, Ontario, Canada.

Jim is a certified coach and actively works with clients to help them realize the need to have strong relationships in their personal, business and spiritual life and works with them to find the love. Also, he is passionate about working with singles to help them realize their desire to enter into a long-term relationship better equipped. To find out more about his coaching go to: www.YourRelationshipRescueCoach.com. For reading this book you are entitled to receive a FREE 30 minute session. In the session you will identify areas that may be sabotaging your relationships, create a crystal clear vision and leave refreshed and renewed ready to move forward. To claim your session email Jim directly at jim@YourRelationshipRescue Coach.com

He is also a licensed wedding officiant in the province of Ontario and loves connecting with couples to work with them on their special day. Also, find out how you can work with the Author to go through the material from this book to help create a strong foundation to build a stronger marriage. To find out more go to: www.JimHetheringtonOfficiant.com or email Jim directly at jim@CelebratingLife.ca.

The author is available for delivering presentations and workshops. For rates and availability please contact the author directly at: jim@YourRelationshipRescueCoach.com.

Be sure to visit www.YourRelationshipRescueCoach.com to find useful articles and resources to help you along your journey.

To order more books, please visit:
www.IncreaseTheLove.com or www.amazon.com.